LITTLE BOOK OF

LONDON

*The Quintessential Guide
to the Royal Capital*

VESNA NESKOW

MAPS BY DAVID LINDROTH INC.

ILLUSTRATED BY
KERREN BARBAS STECKLER

PETER PAUPER PRESS, INC.
WHITE PLAINS, NEW YORK

DEDICATED TO THE MEMORY OF
JOE AND KOSTA, DEAR FRIENDS AND
ADVENTUROUS TRAVELERS

Editor: Mara Conlon
Designed by Heather Zschock
Illustrations copyright © 2013 Kerren Barbas Steckler
London Underground map © 2013 Transport for London
Used with permission.
Neighborhood maps © 2013 David Lindroth, Inc.
Cover: Image of Guards © ICONOTEC
Image of House of Parliament © Brand X Pictures/Media Bakery

Copyright © 2013
Peter Pauper Press, Inc.
202 Mamaroneck Avenue
White Plains, NY 10601
All rights reserved
ISBN 978-1-4413-1355-3
Printed in Hong Kong
7 6 5 4 3 2 1

Visit us at www.peterpauper.com

THE LITTLE
BLACK BOOK OF
LONDON

CONTENTS

INTRODUCTION

The curious mix of tradition and innovation that characterizes London is at the heart of so many of the contradictory forces that have coexisted for two millennia in the soul of the city. It is perhaps this mix that has allowed London to withstand foreign invaders and re-create itself in the face of repeated disasters. The invading armies of Julius Caesar and Claudius took over a small Celtic settlement on the banks of the Thames and there established Londinium, which soon expanded as a mercantile center. By the time of the Norman Conquest of 1066, London was a political, religious, and administrative capital. Destroyed by the plague of 1665 and the Great Fire of 1666, it was rebuilt and not long afterward stood at the forefront of the commercial and industrial booms of the 18th and 19th centuries, when England was a world power with colonies across the globe. Heavily bombed in World War II, the capital again suffered widespread destruction only to rebuild itself yet again and become, by the 1960s, "swinging London," a center of fashion, music, and popular culture.

The capital is situated, in ethos as well as geography, between Europe and America, with ritual and protocol balancing easily with anarchistic independence. The

long monarchist tradition endures in the postmodern age, embodied in the ceremonies and rituals of the royal family and the political establishment. Ornate buildings in the West End, from

Buckingham Palace and Kensington Palace to the Houses of Parliament and Westminster Abbey, attest to a history of power and glory. London's museums, housing some of the world's greatest masterpieces, are themselves part of the city's classical heritage. More recent architectural sites, like the glass addition atop the Victorian Charing Cross station, have bridged eras or created futuristic designs.

Yet the strongest force influencing an expanding world-view has perhaps been exerted by the influx of people from all corners of the globe, many from former British colonies. Settling in the capital, they've not always been welcomed by the English. Nevertheless, London's vibrant ethnic communities give a multicultural richness and brilliance to the city, adding to the wealth of artistic, culinary, and architectural pleasures.

Energy and excitement, edginess and humor give impetus to the innovators, both homegrown and from around the world, that put London at the forefront of art, music, theater, and fashion. The city offers excitement and vitality while its many parks and gardens offer refuge and tranquility.

When setting foot in London, be prepared for an exciting and eclectic journey. From St. Paul's Cathedral to the London Eye, from the Royal Opera House to the Jazz Café, from the British Museum to the Tate Modern, from tea at the Ritz to samosas in Brick Lane, London is an exhilarating ride, filling the visitor with a multitude of experiences. Be prepared to be inspired and enriched.

HOW TO USE THIS GUIDE

The first eight chapters of this guide cover neighborhoods of London. Chapter 9 highlights areas farther from the center, and Chapter 10 presents excursions outside London. Each chapter includes a fold-out map for the areas covered, with color-coded numbers corresponding to the places mentioned in the text. **Red** symbols indicate **Places to See** (landmarks, arts & entertainment). **Blue** symbols indicate **Places to Eat & Drink** (restaurants, cafés, bars, and nightlife). **Orange** symbols indicate **Where to Shop**. **Green** symbols indicate **Where to Stay**. Each place mentioned is followed by its address, telephone number, Web site, and hours, if available.

Here are our keys for restaurant and hotel costs:

Restaurants
Cost of an appetizer and main course without drinks

£	Up to £20
££	£20–£35
£££	£35–£50
££££	£50 and up

Hotels
Cost per room per night

£	Up to £125
££	£125–£225
£££	£225–£350
££££	£350 and up

ALL ABOUT MONEY

Money Changing

Britain's currency is the pound sterling (£): £1 (pound) equals 100p (pence). A "quid" refers to a pound, and pence are often called simply by their letter *p*. Credit cards and ATMs usually give the best exchange rates (but your bank may charge a conversion fee). Banks are the next best. Post offices and exchange kiosks (Bureau de Change) don't give great rates. Airports, hotels, and shops charge exorbitant fees.

Some reliable exchange offices are: **American Express Foreign Exchange Services** (*Heathrow Airport and several branches in London, two of which are: 30-31 Haymarket, 020-7484-9600, hours: M–F 9AM–5:30PM, Sa 9AM–5PM, Tube: Piccadilly Circus; and 40 Great Russell St., 020-7637-0019, Tube: Tottenham Court Rd.; hours: M–F 9AM–5:30PM, Sa 8AM–5PM*); **Thomas Cook Travel** (*1 Marble Arch, 0844-335-7475, Tube: Marble Arch; hours: M–W, F 9AM–7PM, Th 10AM–7PM, Sa 9:30AM–5:30PM, Su 10AM–6PM*).

Tipping

Restaurants usually add a 15% to 20% service charge to your bill, so round up the bill or leave some change. Otherwise, 15% to 20% tips are usual. No tips are given in pubs. In cocktail bars, 75p (or more) to the waiter per round of drinks is customary. Hotels generally add a 10% to 15% service charge to the bill. Tip chambermaids £1/day or more; bellhops, £1/bag. Tip taxi drivers 10% to 15%, but never less than 30p; hairdressers and barbers, 10% to 15%; tour guides, £3.

PUBLIC TRANSPORTATION

Getting to and from the Airport

Flights from the U.S. generally go to London's Heathrow Airport, but more airlines are now flying to Gatwick Airport.

HEATHROW AIRPORT

Heathrow Airport *(Hounslow, west of London, 0844-335-1801, www.heathrowairport.com)* has four terminals. Most U.S. airlines arrive at Terminal 3; European airlines, at Terminals 1 and 2; British Airways transatlantic flights and other long-distance flights, at Terminal 4.

The British Airport Authority's train service **Heathrow Express** *(0845-600-1515, www.heathrowexpress.com)* takes 15 minutes from Heathrow Terminals 1, 2, and 3 to Paddington Station (23 minutes from Terminals 4 & 5) and leaves every 15 minutes (5:10AM to 11:25PM). Cost: adults £20, kids £10; round trip, adults £34, kids £17. Buy tickets from ticket machines at Heathrow or on the train (tickets purchased on the train are usually more expensive). Less expensive but slower is the **Underground** (subway system); it takes 35 to 40 minutes (to South Kensington station on the Piccadilly line) and costs £5.50. **Buses** are also available. More information on Underground and bus connections is available at 0843-222-1234 or the **Transport for London (TfL)**

Web site *(www.tfl.gov.uk/tfl)*. There are **TfL Information Centres** at every Heathrow terminal and at major Underground stations in London. A **taxi** from Heathrow to central London costs approximately £50 to £80 (more during rush hours).

GATWICK AIRPORT

From **Gatwick Airport** *(West Sussex, south of London, 0844-892-0322, www.gatwickairport.com)* the train is the fastest way into the city. **Gatwick Express** *(0845-850-1530, www.gatwickexpress.com)* trains leave for Victoria Station every 15 minutes and take about 30 to 35 minutes to get into the city. Cost: adults £19.90, kids £9.95; round trip, adults £34.90, kids £17.45. **Buses** between Gatwick and Victoria Coach Station (next to Victoria Rail Station) take about 1-1/2 to 2 hours. **National Express** *(0871-781-8178, www.nationalexpress.com)* buses leave about every hour. Cost, one way: £6.50 to £8 depending on the hour. **Taxis** between Gatwick and central London *(Checker Cars, 01293-567-700, www.checkercars.com)* cost about £80 to £90; negotiate the fare first because Gatwick is outside the metropolitan zone.

TRAVEL BETWEEN HEATHROW AND GATWICK

National Express 700 *(0871-781-8178, www.national express.com)* buses leave every 15 to 20 minutes. The trip takes about an hour and costs £25 one way.

Getting Around London

TRANSPORT FOR LONDON (TfL)

TfL *(0843-222-1234, www.tfl.gov.uk)* has Travel Information Centres at Heathrow *(Terminals 1, 2, and 3 Underground station; 7:30AM–7:30PM)* and in London at Liverpool Street Station, Victoria Station, and several other stations throughout the city *(M–Sa 7:15AM–8PM, Su 8:15AM–7PM, hours vary by station).*

THE TUBE

The fastest, most efficient way of getting around London is via the Underground (subway system), colloquially called the Tube, which has six fare zones. Most of central London is in Zone 1. The Zone 1 fare is £4.50. There are 12 different Tube lines. You can find an Underground fold-out map in the back of this book. After entering the Underground, hold on to your ticket—you need it to exit!

The **Oyster card**, a prepaid card, provides significant discounts, depending on zones traveled and time of day. Each Zone 1 trip costs £2.10 for adults, £0.80–£1.05 for kids. The Oyster can be bought online at www.tfl.gov.uk, at tube stations, London travel information centers, some train stations, newsagents, or by calling 0843-222-1234. For visitors, the Oyster is the least expensive way of getting around on public transportation. To use it, simply touch it on a card reader at the beginning and end of your trip.

UNDERGROUND

Travelcards offer discounted fares for mostly unlimited travel on Underground (Zones 1 and 2), buses, and British Rail in Greater London; you need a passport-sized photo to buy one. The **1-Day Travelcard** (Zones 1–2) costs from £8.80 for adults, £4.40 for kids. The **Off-Peak 1-Day Travelcard** (Zones 1–2), valid after 10AM, weekdays only, costs £7.30 for adults, £3.40 for kids. The **7-Day Travelcard** starts at £30.40 for adults and £15.20 for kids. Weekly and monthly **Travelcards** are also available.

BUSES

Most buses operate all day, with fewer running at night. Cash bus fares are £2.40; Oyster fares are £1.40. Single tickets are sold at roadside ticket machines (exact fare required), newsstands, and Underground stations, or use your Travelcard. For more Tube and bus info, go to www.tfl.gov.uk or call 0843-222-1234.

TAXIS

London's famous "black cabs" *(07957-696673, between 10PM–3AM 07904-805508, www.londonblackcabs.co.uk)* are fairly expensive. The minimum fare begins at £2.40, increasing at about £2/mile. Surcharges are added for additional passengers, stowed luggage, trips after 8PM, weekends, and public holidays. Call a cab from **Radio Taxis** *(020-7272-0272, www.radiotaxis.co.uk)* or **Dial-a-Cab** *(cash bookings 020-7253-5000, credit/debit card bookings 020-7426-3420, www.dialacab.co.uk)*.

MINICABS

Car services, or "minicabs," are cheaper than black cabs, but negotiate the fare in advance. Licensed minicab companies include: **Addison Lee** *(0844-800-6677, www.addisonlee.com)*; **Lady Minicabs** *(020-7272-3300, www.ladyminicabs. co.uk)*; and **Abbey Cars** *(020-8969-2777, www.abbey carsuk.co.uk)*.

MAKING PHONE CALLS

To call a London number from within London, dial it as it appears in this guide, including the initial 020, London's main area code, or any of the other area codes. To call from the U.S., dial 011+44 then drop the initial 0 in the 020 area code: i.e., dial 011+44+20+the number. To dial internationally from London, dial 00+country code+area code+number. (For the U.S. and Canada, dial 00+1+area code+number.)

SHOPPING TIPS

Hours: Shops are generally open Monday–Saturday 10AM–6PM. Some stay open late night, until 7PM or 8PM, on Thursdays in the West End and Wednesdays in Chelsea and Knightsbridge. Many shops are open on Sundays, 11AM–5PM or 12PM–6PM.

Sales: January and July are the sale months in London, with great bargains.

Tax Rebates: Non-European Union (EU) citizens can get a refund for the 20% value-added tax (VAT) included in the price of most items. You must spend a certain amount (usually £75) in the store. When you pay, ask for a VAT refund form and envelope from each retailer offering the rebate. You'll have to show your passport. When leaving the U.K. (if traveling elsewhere, at the last EU airport you leave), go to the Tax Refund Desk at the airport's Customs Office. You will have to show your purchases, passport, airline ticket, and refund forms. The official will stamp your forms. Keep your copy and mail the other in the envelope provided. There is a special drop box for these envelopes by the VAT refund desk, but you must have U.K. postage on each envelope if mailing from the U.K. It's best to opt for credit on your credit card, or ask to be mailed a check (but not in pounds; the conversion fee is hefty). This will take up to three months. You might be able to get a cash refund at the airport's Cash VAT Refund desk. If you get a Global Refund form from a store, you can get your refund while still in London from Global Refund's office at the **Britain and London Visitor Centre** *(339 Oxford St., hours: daily 8AM–12PM, 6PM–8PM, www.globalblue.com).*

Tax-Free Shops: Shops with "Tax-Free Shopping" stickers in their windows will deduct the tax if you have a non-EU passport and are leaving the EU within three months. Heathrow Airport also has tax-free shops once past passport control.

ETIQUETTE TIPS

Certain rules of behavior are sacrosanct to Brits of all classes and attitudes. On escalators and moving sidewalks, stand on the right to let people pass on the left. If you're with others, stand in a line on escalator steps, not side by side. And for heaven's sake, don't jump the queue! Brits line up (*queue* up) for just about everything. On subways, let exiting passengers out before you enter the train. Another law of the land is the pedestrian's right of way on a zebra (striped) crossing. If you're not on the zebra, you could get run over; but on those stripes, you're in safe territory. If you notice someone's not abiding by these rules, you can be sure he or she is a foreigner.

"Please," "thank you," and "sorry" are so common that they are sometimes said even when not totally necessary. You will avoid stepping on toes if you respect local custom and use these common courtesies.

ON THE TOWN: FINDING EVENTS & BUYING TICKETS

Booking Tickets: Your best bet is the theater's box office. Agencies such as **Ticketmaster** *(0844-844-0444, www.ticketmaster.co.uk)* and **Keith Prowse** *(www.keith prowse.com)* can charge up to 20% in fees. On the day of the performance, some box offices sell half-price tickets. **Tkts** *(Clocktower building, Leicester Square, Tube: Leicester Square; M–Sa 9AM–7PM, Su 10:30AM–4:30PM, www.tkts.co.uk)* sells discounted tickets on the day of the performance.

Listings: *Time Out*, the weekly magazine, lists just about any event taking place in London. For info on theater, go to *www.officiallondontheatre.co.uk* or *www.london theatre.co.uk*.

Free Concerts: Some churches offer free concerts. **Jazz Plus** *(Victoria Embankment Gardens, Villiers Street, 020-7375-0441, www.alternativearts.co.uk, Tube: Embankment)* has free lunchtime jazz concerts on Tuesdays and Thursdays.

AFTERNOON TEA

The English may not have invented rituals, but they've surely perfected them. Afternoon tea was created in the mid-19th century by Anna, the seventh Duchess of Bedford, one of Queen Victoria's ladies-in-waiting. Too proud to admit being hungry in the middle of the day, she invited her friends for "afternoon tea" and formalized the "rules" of the ritual. Heat the pot before adding the tea, pour boiled water over the tea, drink out of bone china, serve particularly prepared sandwiches and biscuits, and so on. Even Queen Victoria was won over, and a new social event was born!

Today, guidelines for the ritual are set forth by the **Tea Council** *(01483-750599, www.tea.co.uk)*, which hands out a prestigious annual award for the best afternoon tea in London. This is invariably won by luxury hotels. Top hotel restaurants have strict dress codes: jackets and ties for men;

no shorts, sneakers, boat shoes, or sandals. Generally, the more poshly dressed, the better.

Some of the best hotels for high tea are:
Claridge's *(see page 38)*
Brown's Hotel *(see page 38)*
The Dorchester *(see page 38)*
The Ritz *(see page 39)*
St. Martin's Lane *(see page 61)*
The Savoy *(see page 61)*
Sofitel Saint James *(see page 74)*
The Berkeley *(see page 97)*
The Lanesborough *(see page 97)*
Milestone Hotel *(see page 109)*

THAMES CRUISES

River cruises depart from Westminster Pier, next to Westminster Bridge *(Tube: Westminster)*. **Westminster Passenger Service Association** *(020-7930-4721/2062, www.wpsa.co.uk)* runs tours from Westminster to Kew, Richmond, and Hampton Court. **City Cruises** *(020-7740-0400, www.citycruises.com)* offers sightseeing, dinner, and dance cruises.

TOURIST INFORMATION

Web Sites

www.visitbritain.com (tourist info on Britain)
www.visitlondon.com (tourist info on London)
www.freelondonlistings.co.uk (free London events)
www.tfl.gov.uk (info on getting around London)
www.streetmap.co.uk (for street maps of London)
*www.squaremeal.co.uk (restaurants and other
London venues)*
*www.london-discount-hotel.com (info on discounted
rates for hotels)*

Tourist Information Offices

Britain and London Visitor Centre: www.visitbritain.com
City of London Information Centre: St. Paul's Churchyard,
020-7332-1456, www.visitlondon.com, Tube: St. Paul's;
hours: M–Sa 9:30AM–5:30PM, Su 10AM–4PM
London Information Centre: Leicester Sq., 020-7292-2333,
Tube: Leicester Sq., www.londoninformationcentre.com;
hours: daily 8AM–12AM

Information offices are also located at: Heathrow
Airport *(Terminals 1, 2, and 3 Tube stations)*; Gatwick
Airport; Waterloo Station International Terminal;
Victoria Coach Station; Paddington Station. In the
U.S.: **Visit Britain**, 845 Third Ave., 10th Floor, New
York, NY 10022, 800-462-2748.

SEASONAL & SPECIAL EVENTS

Year-Round:

Changing of the Guards (11AM)—Every day (except Sundays) in the summer (May–July), and every other day in the winter, the rotation of the Queen's Guard takes place in the Forecourt of Buckingham Palace *(Buckingham Palace, 020-7930-4832, Palace visit ticket sales at 020-7766-7300, www. royal.gov.uk, www.royalcollection.org.uk, Tube: Green Park, St. James's Park, or Victoria).*

Ceremony of the Keys (9:30PM)—Tower of London entrances are locked by the Yeoman Warders every night in a 700-year-old ceremony; apply three months in advance. See Web site *(Tower of London, Tower Hill, 0844-482-7777, www.hrp.org.uk, Tube: Tower Hill).*

Gun Salutes are fired to commemorate historical events. They take place on the following days: **February 6**, Accession Day; **April 21**, Queen's birthday; **June 2**, Coronation Day; **June 10**, Duke of Edinburgh's birthday; **mid–late November**, State Opening of Parliament (in Green Park). You can see them at **noon**: King's Troop Royal Horse Artillery charges on horseback through Hyde Park and fires a 41-gun salute opposite the Dorchester Hotel, and at **1PM**: see the 62-gun salute, Tower of London, Honourable Artillery Company. For additional dates and ceremonies, check the British Monarchy Web site, *www.royal.gov.uk.*

Spring:

Oxford & Cambridge Boat Race (March/April) *Thames, from Putney to Mortlake, www.theboatrace.org, Tube: Putney Bridge.*

London Marathon (April) *Greenwich Park to the Mall, 020-7902-0200, www.london-marathon.co.uk, Tube: Charing Cross.*

Chelsea Flower Show (May) *Royal Hospital, Royal Hospital Road, Chelsea, ticket bookings online only, www.rhs.org.uk, Tube: Sloane Square.*

May Fayre & Puppet Festival (May) *St. Paul's Church Garden, Bedford Street, Covent Garden, 020-7375-0441, www.alternativearts.co.uk, Tube: Covent Garden.*

Summer:

City of London Festival (June–July)—Concerts, exhibits, readings, dance, theater, talks *(several venues in the city, box office 0845-120-7502, www.colf.org).*

Henley Royal Regatta (Five days in June/July) *(Henley-on-Thames, Oxfordshire, 01491-572-153, www.hrr.co.uk, trains available from Paddington Station).*

Kew Summer Festival (June–September)—Various events and special activities; visit Web site for specific details *(Royal Botanic Gardens, Kew, Richmond, Surrey, 020-8332-5655, www.kew.org, Tube: Kew Gardens).*

Trooping the Colour (mid-June)—Official celebration of Queen Elizabeth's birthday. Queen leaves Buckingham Palace for Horse Guards Parade (10AM) and then returns to palace for Royal Air Force flyby (1PM) and gun salute from Green Park *(Horse Guards Parade, Whitehall, Westminster, 020-7930-3070, www.trooping-the-colour.co.uk, www.royal.gov.uk, Tube: Westminster, Charing Cross).*

Wimbledon Lawn Tennis Championships (June/July) *Church Road, Wimbledon, 020-8944-1066, M–F 9AM–5PM, www.wimbledon.com, Tube: Southfields.*

Coin Street Festival (June–September)—Music, dance, and folk art of London's diverse communities *(South Bank, 020-7021-1600, www.coinstreet.org, Tube: Southwark, Waterloo).*

Spitalfields Festival (June)—Old and new music in fab Christ Church Spitalfields *(main venue at Christ Church Spitalfields, Commercial Street, 020-7377-1362, www.spitalfieldsmusic.org.uk, Tube: Liverpool Street; phone box office hours: M–F 10AM–6PM).*

Jazz Plus (June–July) *Victoria Embankment Gardens, Villiers St., 020-7375-0441, www.alternativearts.co.uk.*

The Proms (July–September)—One of the world's greatest orchestral music festivals *(Royal Albert Hall, Kensington Gore, South Kensington, 0845-401-5040/5; daily 9AM–9PM, www.bbc.co.uk/proms, Tube: South Kensington, High Street Kensington).*

Great British Beer Festival (August)— Samplings of more than 450 ales, lagers, ciders, perries, and foreign beers *(Earls Court, 01727-867-201, www.camra.org.uk, Tube: Earl's Court).*

Autumn:

Open House London (September)—Some 750 palaces, private homes, and offices open to the public; free admission. Apply for a buildings guide in August; book ahead for some venues *(locations throughout London, 020-3006-7008, www.openhouselondon.org, www.open-city.org.uk).*

London Film Festival (October–November) *Several venues throughout the city, 020-7928-3232, www.lff.org.uk, www.bfi.org.uk.*

London Jazz Festival (November) *London clubs and concert halls, 020-7324-1880, www.serious. org.uk.*

State Opening of Parliament (November or December)— Queen goes to Parliament in royal coach with Household Cavalry to open Parliament; televised ceremony on BBC *(Palace of Westminster, Westminster, 020-7219-3000, House of Commons 020-7219-4272, House of Lords 020-7219-3107, www.parliament.uk, Tube: Westminster).*

Winter:

Olympia London International Horse Show (December) *Olympia Exhibition Halls, Hammersmith Road, Kensington, tickets: 0871-230-5580, www.olympiahorse show.com.*

London Art Fair (January)—Modern British and contemporary artists' fair *(Business Design Centre, 52 Upper Street, Islington, 020-7359-3535, 020-7288-6456, www.londonartfair.co.uk, Tube: Angel).*

International Tourist Guide Day (February)—Tourists are invited to participate in samples of walks, talks, and tours by professional tourist guides, free of charge *(several venues, 020-7403-1115, www.blue-badge.org.uk).*

LONDON'S TOP PICKS

London offers an abundance of one-of-a-kind attractions and experiences for visitors. Here are 14 of the top picks not to be missed!

TOP PICK!

chapter 1

MAYFAIR

SOHO & TRAFALGAR SQUARE

COVENT GARDEN &
THE STRAND

MAYFAIR
SOHO & TRAFALGAR SQUARE
COVENT GARDEN & THE STRAND

Places to See:

1. Shepherd Market
2. Berkeley Square
3. St. George's Gardens
4. Church of the Immaculate Conception
5. Grosvenor Square
6. Hanover Square
7. Burlington Arcade
8. Regent Street
9. Royal Academy of Arts
10. Faraday Museum
11. Handel House Museum
43. London Palladium
44. Liberty
45. Carnaby Street
46. Broadwick Street
47. Berwick Street
48. French House
49. Soho Square
50. Old Compton Street
51. Shaftesbury Avenue
52. Gerrard Street
53. Leicester Square
54. Piccadilly Circus
55. TRAFALGAR SQUARE ★
56. St. Martin-in-the-Fields
57. NATIONAL GALLERY ★

58. National Portrait Gallery
59. Theatre Royal Haymarket
60. Soho Theatre
61. Photographers' Gallery
92. Covent Garden Piazza
93. St. Paul's Covent Garden
94. Royal Opera House
95. Neal Street
96. Neal's Yard
97. Seven Dials
98. London Coliseum
99. Adelphi Theatre
100. Somerset House
101. Victoria Embankment Gardens
102. Cleopatra's Needle
103. London's Transport Museum
104. Donmar Warehouse
105. Novello Theatre

★ *Top Pick*

Places to Eat & Drink:

12. The Grill
13. Richoux
14. Sketch
15. Chor Bizarre
16. Claridge's
17. The Promenade
18. The English Tea Room
19. Amaranto Lounge
20. The Palm Court
21. Guinea
22. Ye Grapes
23. Shepherd's Tavern
62. Imli Restaurant
63. Red Fort
64. Patisserie Valerie
65. Maison Bertaux
66. Yauatcha
67. Ronnie Scott's
68. The 100 Club
69. Borderline
70. Bar Italia
71. Albannach
72. Bar Rumba
73. Jewel
75. Shadow Lounge
106. J. Sheekey
107. The Ivy
108. Savoy Grill
109. Rules
110. Tom's Kitchen
111. Tom's Terrace
112. Poetry Café
113. Gordon's Wine Bar

114. Lamb and Flag
115. 12 Bar Club
116. Lobby Bar
117. Heaven

Where to Shop:

7. Burlington Arcade
8. Regent Street
24. Bond Street
25. Asprey
26. Fenwick
27. South Molton Street
28. Elemis Day Spa
29. Savile Row
30. Ozwald Boateng
31. Bruton Street
32. Hatchards
33. Waterstone's Piccadilly
34. John Lewis
35. Debenhams
44. Liberty
45. Carnaby Street
45. Broadwick Street
76. A Bathing Ape
77. Newburgh Street
78. Maharishi
80. Agent Provocateur
81. Berwick Street Market
82. Vintage House
83. Foyles
84. Blackwell
85. Henry Pordes Books
95. Neal Street
96. Neal's Yard

MAYFAIR

Bond Street, Green Park, Hyde Park Corner, Piccadilly Circus

• SNAPSHOT •

Mayfair is among the most prestigious addresses of London, with elegant Georgian homes, well-tended squares, decorous embassies, and glamorous high-fashion designer shops. Park Lane, facing Hyde Park, boasts some of London's most luxurious hotels, which replaced the town mansions of estate owners, such as the Duke of Westminster and the Earl of Northbrook.

The area got its name from a rowdy 17th-century fair that took place there every May, so wayward, in fact, that it was closed down in 1706. Architect Edward Shepherd later turned the site into a food market and built small houses around the square. This came to be known as Shepherd Market.

Today the tony shops, restaurants, and bars of Mayfair cater to the wealthy—and those looking for jet-set glamour. Old shops and galleries mingle with auction houses and international designer-label shops. A walk through this staid neighborhood reveals gems of old London

homes: Georgian houses and brick buildings encircle green oases such as Berkeley and Grosvenor Squares.

PLACES TO SEE
Landmarks:

The heart of Mayfair is **Shepherd Market (1)** *(between Curzon/Shepherd Sts.)*, surrounded by Edward Shepherd's 18th-century houses. A pedestrian haven, the site bursts with charming cafés, restaurants, and shops. **Berkeley Square (2)** *(at Bruton/Hill Sts. and Berkeley/Davies Sts.)* is a fabulous green expanse shaded by giant plane trees and encircled by dignified Georgian houses. Less exposed, **St. George's Gardens (3)** *(also known as Mount Street Gardens, off Mount St. and Carlos Place)* is hidden by plane trees, Queen Anne houses, and wrought-iron gates. In one corner, the wonderful, ornate **Church of the Immaculate Conception (4)** *(114 Mount St., 020-7493-7811, www. farmstreet.org.uk; call for hours)*, the "Farm Street Church," is where writer Graham Greene went to confess adultery; he seemed to take well to absolution because he made repeated visits there!

A few blocks north, **Grosvenor Square (5)** *(between South Audley/Duke Sts.)* is dominated by the U.S. Embassy, a gray hulk out of sync with the neighborhood. The statues of Franklin D. Roosevelt and Dwight D. Eisenhower are more interesting aesthetically. Another green expanse is **Hanover Square (6)** *(at Hanover/Brook Sts.)*. Nearby, **St. George's Church**, an 18th-century wedding chapel, is where George Eliot, Teddy Roosevelt, and other celebrities said "I do."

Burlington Arcade (7) *(between Burlington Gdns./Piccadilly, 020-7493-1764, www.burlington-arcade.co.uk)*, one of several early 19th-century skylight-covered promenades of shops, emulates ornate Parisian arcades of the time. Decorum is enforced by patrols of beadles empowered to throw out anyone who disrupts the reserved atmosphere in the arcade. Majestic **Regent Street (8)**, a grand curving thoroughfare, was designed by architect John Nash in the early 19th century. The beautiful white Regency buildings give the street its sweeping splendor.

Arts & Entertainment:

The **Royal Academy of Arts (9)** *(Burlington House, Piccadilly, 020-7300-8000, www.royalacademy.org.uk; hours: Sa–Th 10AM–6PM, F 10AM–10PM)* mounts inter-

esting, eclectic exhibits. For 200 years the Summer Exhibition has culled work from the public at large. Michael Faraday, the 19th-century scientist and inventor who helped shape the Industrial Revolution and the Modern Age, is celebrated at the **Faraday Museum (10)** *(Royal Institution, 21 Albemarle St., 020-7409-2992, www.rigb.org; hours: reception M–F 9AM–6PM)*. Faraday, a celebrity in his time, invented the electric motor, transformer, and generator.

German composer George Frideric Handel lived in what is now the **Handel House Museum (11)** *(25 Brook St., entrance in back in Lancashire Court, 020-7495-1685, www.handelhouse.org; hours: Tu, W, F, Sa 10AM–6PM, Th 10AM–8PM, Su 12PM–6PM)*. It holds

Thursday evening baroque music recitals, weekend activities for kids, and lively programs (e.g., the Beer & Baroque evening). Much later, Jimi Hendrix lived briefly next door (at 23 Brook St.).

PLACES TO EAT & DRINK
Where to Eat:

Most Mayfair restaurants are very expensive. **The Grill (12) (££-££££)** *(The Dorchester, 53 Park Ln., 020-7629-8888, www.thedorchester.com; hours: M–F 7AM–10:30AM, 12PM–2:30PM, 6:30PM–10:30PM, Sa 8AM–11AM, 12:30PM–3PM, 6:30PM–11PM, Su 8AM–11AM, 12:30PM–3:30PM, 7PM–10:30PM)* is known for its luxury and refinement, its traditional service and setting, and its very British roast beef, Scottish lobster, and Yorkshire pudding. If you're hungry in Mayfair without a trust fund to fall back on, **Richoux (13) (£-££)** *(41a South Audley St., 020-7629-5228, www.richoux.co.uk; hours: M–F 7:30AM–11PM, Sa 7:30AM–11:30PM, Su 9AM–10PM)* is a great, reliable tearoom. An upscale chain, it serves good traditional English breakfast and tea while lunch and dinner are more Continental. The ambience is Mayfairishly delightful, from doily to tea cozy!

Stunningly theatrical, **Sketch (14) (££-££££)** *(9 Conduit St., 020-7659-4500, www.sketch.uk.com; call for hours & showtimes)* is the brainchild of epicurean restaurateur Mourad Mazouz and celebrity chef Pierre Gagnaire. This high-concept, high-style venue includes a parlor, two bars, two restaurants, an art gallery, and a lecture hall. Chic, extravagant, and extremely expensive, it is the most innovative dining spot in London. With an unusual décor, from four-poster beds converted into tables to carved wooden chairs cushioned in exotic fabrics, **Chor Bizarre (15)** (£-£££) *(16 Albemarle St., 020-7629-9802/8542, www.chorbizarrerestaurant.com; hours: M-Sa 12PM-3PM, 6PM-11:30PM, Su 6PM-10:30PM)* offers more than Indian cuisine; it's a cornucopia of food and objects inspired by the Indian "Chor Bazaar," or "thieves' market."

Mayfair is decidedly the address for posh British afternoon tea. The most traditional high tea, in terms of both food and ritual, is served at the luxury hotels: **Claridge's (16)** (£££-££££) *(Brook St., 020-7629-8860, www.claridges.co.uk; hours: tea served daily 3PM, 3:30PM, 5PM, 5:30PM, reservations needed 020-7107-8886)*; **The Promenade (17)** (£££-££££) *(at The Dorchester, 53 Park Lane, 020-7629-8888, www.thedorchester.com; hours: tea served daily 1:15PM, 2:30PM, 3:15PM, 4:45PM, 5:15PM)*; **The English Tea Room (18)** (£££-££££) *(at Brown's Hotel, 30-34 Albemarle St., 020-7493-6020, www.brownshotel.com; hours: tea served M-Th 3PM-6PM, F 2PM-6PM, Sa-Su 12PM-6:30PM)*; **Amaranto Lounge (19)** (£££-££££) *(at the Four Seasons Hotel London, Hamilton Place, Park Ln., 020-7499-0888, www.fourseasons.com; hours: tea served daily 3PM-6PM)*; **The Palm Court (20)** (£££-££££) *(at The Ritz, 150 Piccadilly, 020-7300-2345, www.theritzlondon.com; hours: tea served daily 11:30AM, 1:30PM, 3:30PM, 5:30PM, 7:30PM, reserve 12 weeks in advance)*.

Bars & Nightlife:

The glitterati have drinks at sybaritic **Sketch (14)** *(see page 33)*. Besides its grill, the **Guinea (21)** *(30 Bruton Pl., 020-7409-1728, www.theguinea.co.uk; hours: M–F 11:30AM–10:30PM, Sa 12PM–11PM)* has a jovial old-world pub established in the 15th century to tend to the servants of the wealthy, whose horses were stabled in the mews next door. It has resisted the glitz and glamour of Mayfair, but its small, dark bar is full of atmosphere and is a trendy spot. Other good pubs in the area are **Ye Grapes (22)** *(16 Shepherd Market, 020-7493-4216; hours: M–F 11AM–11PM, Sa 11:30AM–11PM, Su 12PM–10:30PM)* and **Shepherd's Tavern (23)** *(50 Hertford St., 020-7499-3017; hours: M–Sa 11AM–11PM, Su 12PM–10:30PM)*.

WHERE TO SHOP

Mayfair has the most upscale designer shopping in town—stunning, elegant, shocking, dramatic, and expensive. Since the mid-1800s, Bond Street (24) has been synonymous with high fashion. Beau Brummel strutted up and down the street, letting potential customers eye his clothes. Today, you'll find high fashion houses there: Prada, Hermès, Armani, Louis Vuitton, Donna Karan, Calvin Klein, and Nicole Farhi, among others, are on New Bond (northern part) and Old Bond (southern) streets.

Asprey (25) *(167 New Bond St., 020-7493-6767, www.asprey.com; hours: M–Sa 10AM–6PM)* is a must-see, both for its architectural beauty (architect Sir Norman Foster and interior designer David Mlinaric joined five 18th-century houses) and its luxury goods (designer ready-to-wear, its own label, and lovely jewelry). If luxury items are beyond your reach, check out **Fenwick (26)** *(63 New Bond St., 020-7629-9161, www.fenwick.co.uk; hours: M–W, F–Sa 10AM–6:30PM, Th 10AM–8PM, Su 12PM–6PM)*, a chic, more affordable department store.

South Molton Street (27) is home to the famed **Browns** *(24-27 South Molton St., 020-7514-0016, www.brownsfashion. com; hours: M–Sa 10AM–6:30PM, Th to 7PM)*, featuring international designers. **Browns Focus** *(38-39 South Molton St., 020-7514-0063, www.brownsfashion. com; hours: M–Sa 10AM–6:30PM, Th to 7PM)* showcases new young designers. The exotic **Elemis Day Spa (28)** *(2-3 Lancashire Court, 020-7499-4995, www.elemis.com; hours: M–F 10AM–9PM, Sa 9AM–9PM, Su 10AM–6PM)* offers divine skin and body treatments for women and men; their skin-care line is extraordinary.

In exclusive **Savile Row (29)**, royally appointed tailors have been outfitting gentlemen for centuries, and more contemporary menswear designers have introduced a youthful air. The custom-made suits of **Henry Poole & Co.** *(15 Savile Row, 020-7734-5985, www.henrypoole.com)* have clothed the likes of Napoleon Bonaparte, Charles Dickens, Winston Churchill, and Charles de Gaulle. The offices of **Apple Records** once stood at 3 Savile Row. The Beatles played their last concert on the building's rooftop in February 1969. **Ozwald Boateng (30)** *(30 Savile Row, 020-7437-2030, www.ozwaldboateng.co.uk)* gives an imaginative twist to the classic British men's suit; his custom designs are the rage of London.

Check out **Bruton Street (31)** and **Bruton Place**. It's hard to miss the bold, sexy designs of **Matthew Williamson** *(28 Bruton St., 020-7629-6200, www.matthewwilliamson.co.uk; hours: M–W, F–Sa 10AM–6PM, Th 10AM–7PM)*, especially when worn by clients Sarah Jessica Parker, Gwyneth Paltrow, Kate Moss, and Madonna. Next door, the feminine designs of **Stella McCartney** *(30 Bruton St., 020-7518-3100, www.stellamccartney.com; hours: M–Sa 10AM–7PM)*, both form-fitting and loosely draped, have flattering effects. Don't miss cutting-edge shoe designer **Rupert Sanderson** *(19 Bruton Pl., 020-7491-2260, www.rupertsanderson.com; hours: M–Sa 10AM–6:30PM)*.

The great **Hatchards (32)** *(187 Piccadilly, 020-7439-9921, www.hatchards.co.uk; hours: M–Sa 9:30AM–7PM, Su 12PM–6PM)* is London's oldest bookstore. But **Waterstone's Piccadilly (33)** *(203-206 Piccadilly, 0843-290-8549, www.waterstones.co.uk; hours: M–Sa 9AM–10PM, Su 11:30AM–6PM)*, in a great Art Deco building, is the largest bookstore in Europe. The hip top-floor café has spectacular views. The shops in **Burlington Arcade (7)** *(see also page 32, www.burlington-arcade.co.uk)* sell leather goods, clothing, and jewelry. Check out **Lulu Guinness** (No. 42) for her witty handbags and accessories; **Crockett and Jones** (No. 20-21) make classical English shoes for men and women; and **Vilebrequin** (No. 1-2) stock men's swimwear and casual clothes from St. Tropez, France.

Oxford Street is a jumble of stores and crowds. John Lewis (34) *(278-306 Oxford St., 020-7629-7711, www.johnlewis.com; hours: M–W, F–Sa 9:30AM–8PM, Th 9:30AM–9PM, Su 12PM–6PM)* is noted for china, glass, and housewares. Debenhams (35) *(334-348 Oxford St., 0844-561-6161, www.debenhams.com; hours: M, Tu, Sa 9:30AM–8PM, W 10AM–9PM, Th–F 9:30AM–9PM, Su 12PM–6:30PM)* carries less expensive collections of British designers, such as Jasper Conran, Ben De Lisi, and Julien Macdonald. **Regent Street (8)** is full of stores, from low-cost women's clothing chains **Zara** and **Mango** to **Jaeger** and **Aquascutum** (traditional tailoring), **Lawley's** (china), and **Lush** (bath and beauty). **Molton Brown** *(227 Regent St., 020-7493-7319, www.molton brown.co.uk; hours: M–Sa 10AM–8PM, Su 11AM–6PM)* produces great cosmetics.

WHERE TO STAY

There are probably more luxury hotels per square foot in Mayfair than in any other area. Exclusive, distinguished, and discreet, Claridge's (36) **(££££)** *(Brook St., 020-7629-8860, www.claridges.co.uk)* rooms are Art Deco or Victorian, with modern details in the common areas— a favorite of world leaders and nobility. James Brown, Lord Byron's butler, founded **Brown's Hotel (37) (£££-££££)** *(30-34 Albemarle St., 020-7493-6020, www.brownshotel. com)* in 1837. With Edwardian stained-glass windows and oak paneling, Brown's is legendary.

One of the fabulous luxury hotels of Park Lane, **The Dorchester (38) (£££-££££)** *(53 Park Ln., 020-7629-*

8888, www.thedorchester.com) is fantastically elegant yet relaxed. Brad Pitt, George Clooney, Oprah Winfrey, and Nelson Mandela, among others, swear by it. The **Metropolitan (39)** *(£££-££££)* *(19 Old Park Ln., info: 020-7447-1000, reservations: 020-7447-1047, www.metropolitan.co.uk)* offers a modern minimalist alternative to Park Lane abundance. Not so **The Ritz (40)** *(££££)* *(150 Piccadilly, 020-7493-8181, www.theritz london.com)*, which gave us the word meaning "opulently glamorous." Synonymous with wealth and sophistication, it is ornate, with chandeliers, rococo mirrors, marble columns, high vaulted ceilings, and rooms in Louis XVI style. Not for the faint of heart.

For prolonged stays, **5 Maddox Street (41)** *(£££-££££)* *(5 Maddox St., 020-7647-0200, www.no5maddoxst.com)* provides elegant suites on a daily, weekly, or monthly basis (rates are on a sliding scale). Terraces, rooftop views of the city, indoor staircases, and kitchens add to its Zen-like serenity. For more affordable luxury, **The May Fair (42)** *(£££-££££)* *(Stratton St., 020-7629-7777, www.themay fairhotel.co.uk)* is another choice in an area of luxury hotels.

🚇 *Piccadilly Circus, Leicester Square,*
Tottenham Court Road, Charing Cross

● SNAPSHOT ●

In the center of the West End is Soho, once a slum and a neighborhood of workers and artisans. A cauldron of refugees, Soho began to welcome foreigners fleeing oppression in the 17th century. Greeks, Huguenots, and anti-Revolutionary French were followed by Italian, Spanish, Swiss, and Chinese immigrants. Soho, home to London's Chinatown, is full of French, Greek, and Chinese restaurants and pubs.

Soho is also London's theater and jazz district and the heart of the gay scene. In the 1960s it was the ultimate in hipness, with Carnaby Street deemed the height of cool. Soho still buzzes with appealing cafés, restaurants, and pubs. Here and there, the quarter is also dotted with sex shops and strip joints, rip-off relics of Soho's seedy past. It is this tension between the chic and flashy, creative and seedy, fashionable and déclassé, and Soho's constantly adapting character, that make the quarter intriguing.

South of Soho, Trafalgar Square is one of London's most famous sites, with Nelson's Column a reminder of the nation's powerful military and maritime past. Designed by architect superstar John Nash in the early-19th century, the square is a common meeting point for public gatherings.

PLACES TO SEE
Landmarks:

In 1963 The Beatles first performed live for TV at the **London Palladium (43)** *(8 Argyll St., box office: 0844-412-2957, www.londonpalladium.org)*. The mock-Tudor façade of **Liberty (44)** *(210-220 Regent St., 020-7734-1234, www.liberty.co.uk; hours: M–Sa 10AM–8PM, Su 12PM–6PM)* is hard to miss. Its gables, wood interiors, and fabulous mezzanine give it a country mansion look. Established in 1875 by Arthur Lasenby Liberty, the shop was soon at the forefront of the Arts and Crafts movement, with Liberty prints and William Morris designs. The store continues to promote arts and crafts. In the '60s, **Carnaby Street (45)** *(www.carnaby.co.uk)* was synonymous with "mod." Its fashions again draw the younger crowd.

Poet William Blake was born on **Broadwick Street (46)**, but Doctor John Snow became its celebrity in 1854 by curbing the cholera outbreak. He suspected polluted water and shut down the street's water pump, saving countless lives. A replica of the handleless water pump stands in his memory outside the **John Snow Pub** *(39 Broadwick St., 020-7437-1344; hours: daily 12PM–11PM)*. **Berwick Street (47)** is famous for its fruit and veggie market and specialty food shops. Other wares are also abundant: prostitutes ply their trade from shabby stairwells. Strip joints in the area make grand claims but are really just rip-offs.

Dean Street was full of bohemian hangouts; Dylan Thomas's drinking stints at the York Minster were fabled. The pub is now called **French House (48)** *(49 Dean St., 020-7437-2477/2799, www.frenchhouse soho.com; call for hours)* in honor of its most famous regulars, Charles de Gaulle and his Free French Forces pals, as well as Maurice Chevalier. Karl Marx lived at No. 28 & No. 44 for a while. **Soho Square (49)** lies at the northern edge of the quarter, encircled by advertising and film company offices. **Old Compton Street (50)** is the hub of Soho's gay district. The pedestrian-friendly street is a constant party, friendly and full of gay bars and throngs of hip sybarites. **Shaftesbury Avenue (51)** is marked by grand Victorian theater houses, part of London's famed theater district. It borders on **Chinatown**, whose main artery, **Gerrard Street (52)**, is lined with Chinese restaurants, shops, and residences.

Leicester Square (53) was once a fashionable residential area. Isaac Newton lived there, as did Joshua Reynolds (who became rich painting portraits of the upper class) and William Hogarth. When Soho became a slum, the aristocracy moved out, and the square has remained drab ever since. However, its **tkts booth** sells discounted theater tickets on the day of the show. Nearby, **Piccadilly Circus (54)**, gloriously designed by John Nash, is now a gaudy mix of fast-food joints, tacky tourist shops, and minimalls. The **Eros statue** honors the Earl of Shaftesbury's efforts to curb child labor and improve housing conditions.

John Nash's majestic ★**TRAFALGAR SQUARE** (55), a monument to Britain's naval power, focuses on **Nelson's Column**, built by E. H.

Baily in 1843. Admiral Lord Nelson died in the 1805 Battle of Trafalgar, victoriously fighting Napoleon. The square is located on the grounds of what used to be horse stables dating from the 1400s. Although John Nash originally conceived the idea for the square, the design was somewhat altered by Sir Charles Barry, who styled it after the Italian palazzo. As such, it is very much a favorite public space for Londoners. Street performers entertain and pigeons pester the natives and tourists who linger there, soaking in the city energy. It's the site of many demonstrations, parades, and services. During the Christmas season, a festive tree—an annual gift from Norway—is erected in the square. Don't miss the early 18th-century church of **St. Martin-in-the-Fields (56)** *(Trafalgar Sq., 020-7766-1100, www.stmartin-in-the-fields.org; hours: M, Tu, F 8:30AM–1PM, 2PM–6PM, W 8:30AM–1:15PM, 2PM–5PM, Th 8:30AM–1:15PM, 2PM–6PM, Sa 9:30AM–6PM, Su 3:30PM–5PM, evening concerts; Brass Rubbing Centre, 020-7766-1122, M–W 10AM–6PM, Th–Sa 10AM–8PM, Su 11:30AM–5PM)*, the prototype for Colonial-style churches in the U.S. In World War I, the church provided shelter to soldiers and the homeless; in World War II, it was an air raid shelter; and today it has a soup kitchen for the homeless. Two majestic thoroughfares culminate in

Trafalgar Square: **Whitehall** leads to Westminster Palace, and **The Mall** connects Trafalgar to Buckingham Palace, via the Admiralty Arch.

Arts & Entertainment:

Great masters from the Renaissance through the 19th century comprise the impressive collection of art at the ★**NATIONAL GALLERY (57)** *(Trafalgar Sq., 020-7747-2885, www.nationalgallery.org.uk; hours: daily 10AM–6PM, F till 9PM)*. It contains over 2,300 paintings and is considered one of the finest European museums in the world. If you want to view the collection chronologically, start in the Sainsbury Wing, which covers works from 1260 to 1510. There you can experience pieces from masters such as Pisanello, Gentile da Fabriano, Botticelli, Mantegna, and Bellini. Proceed into the West Wing to view Italian, Dutch, Flemish, and German paintings from 1510 to 1600, including works by Leonardo da Vinci and Sebastiano del Piombo. The North Wing spans the period from 1600 to 1700, highlighting works from Rembrandt (two whole rooms dedicated to just his creations), Vermeer, Van Dyck, Caravaggio, Turner, and Velázquez, among others. And finally, paintings from 1700 to 1900 are housed in

the East Wing, including Venetian, French, German, and English works. Monet's famous *Water Lilies* is on display, as well as van Gogh's *Sunflowers*. Next door, the **National Portrait Gallery (58)** *(2 St. Martin's Pl., 020-7306-0055, www.npg.org. uk; hours: Sa–W 10AM–6PM, Th–F*

$10AM$–$9PM$) gives an intimate glimpse into British history, culture, society, and politics through portraits of important people.

Shaftesbury Avenue (51) and the **Trafalgar Square (55)** area are home to several famous theaters. **Theatre Royal Haymarket (59)** *(18 Suffolk St., Haymarket, box office: 020-7930-8800, www.trh.co.uk; call for showtimes)* is as notable for its architecture as its plays. The respected **Soho Theatre (60)** *(21 Dean St., 020-7478-0100, www.sohotheatre.com; box office hours: M–Sa $10AM$–$10PM$)* is the place for new playwrights. **St. Martin-in-the-Fields (56)** *(see page 43, concert box office: 020-7766-1100)* holds classical music concerts *($7:30PM$)* in a romantic candlelit setting. Free lunchtime recitals *(M, Tu, F, $1PM$)* are the best bargain in town.

The **Photographers' Gallery (61)** *(16-18 Ramillies St., 020-7087-9300, www.thephotographersgallery.org.uk; hours: M–Sa $10AM$–$6PM$, Th til $8PM$, Su $11:30AM$–$6PM$)* is the city's top exhibition space for photography.

PLACES TO EAT & DRINK
Where to Eat:
Modern meets traditional at trendy **Imli Restaurant (62) (£-££)** *(167-169 Wardour St., 020-7287-4243, www.imli.co.uk; hours: M–Sa $12PM$–$11PM$, Su $12PM$–$10PM$)*, where Indian food is served tapas style; the chef gives cooking classes *(Sa $10AM$–$12:30PM$)*. Elegant Indian dining at **Red Fort (63) (£-£££)** *(77 Dean St., 020-7437-2525, www.redfort.co.uk; hours: M–F $12PM$–$3PM$, $5:30PM$–$11:30PM$, Sa $5:30PM$–$11:30PM$, Su $5:30PM$–$10:30PM$)*,

named after Delhi's Red Fort (the Mughal palace of Shah Jahan), is a luxurious experience. Chef Azadur Rahman specializes in Mughal Court cuisine whose refined yet innovative dishes have delighted the palates of royalty, celebrities, and intellectuals. The downstairs cocktail lounge, Zenna *(www.zenna-bar.co.uk; hours: Tu–Sa 5PM–late)*, is another treat.

Patisserie Valerie (64) (£) *(44 Old Compton St., 020-7437-3466, www.patisserie-valerie.co.uk; hours: M–Tu 7:30AM–9PM, W–F 7:30AM–11PM, Sa 8AM–11PM, Su 9AM–9PM)*, the classic French bistro, has sublime pastries and so-so food. At another Soho classic, **Maison Bertaux (65) (£)** *(28 Greek St., 020-7437-6007, www.maison bertaux.com; hours: M–Sa 8:30AM–11PM, Su 9:30AM–8PM)*, great croissants and fabulous pastries complement the fabulous blends of tea. The epicurean dim sum delights of **Yauatcha (66) (££-£££)** *(15 Broadwick St., 020-7494-8888, www.yauatcha.com; hours: M–Sa 12PM–11:30PM, Su 12PM–10:30PM)* are matched by its simple elegance and stylishness. Christian Liaigre designed the interior, while chef Cheong Wah Soon designs the Cantonese menu. The uniforms were created by Tom Yip, costume designer for *Crouching Tiger, Hidden Dragon*. The tearoom's futuristic interior, visible from outside, often draws the curious to explore.

Bars & Nightlife:

Ronnie Scott's (67) *(47 Frith St., 020-7439-0747, www.ronniescotts.co.uk; hours: M–Sa 6PM–3AM, Su 12PM–4PM, 6:30PM–12AM)*, the London mecca of jazz, might be the most famous jazz club in the world.

Stan Getz, Bill Evans, Ben Webster, and Zoot Sims are among the top-notch musicians who have played there. The Rolling Stones once played at **The 100 Club (68)** *(100 Oxford St., 020-7636-0933, www.the100club. co.uk; call for hours)*, another jazz venue. Good new rock and pop bands hit the small basement bar **Borderline (69)** *(Orange Yard, off Manette St., 020-7734-5547, mamacolive.com/theborderline; call for hours)*. **Bar Italia (70)** *(22 Frith St., 020-7437-4520, www.baritalia soho.co.uk; daily 7AM–5AM)* is an Italian neighborhood classic, decked out with the requisite Rocky Marciano poster, red leatherette bar stools, and Formica counter-tops. French Resistance leaders went to the **French House (48)** *(see page 42)* to quaff a few glasses of *vin rouge* after a hard day of resisting. Surrounded by traditional and trendy pubs and cafés, it wears its shabby character with pride and is rewarded by the crowds that elbow their way in. The Scottish theme at **Albannach (71)** *(66 Trafalgar Sq., 020-7930-0066, www.albannach.co.uk; hours: Th–F 7PM–1AM, Sa 9PM–3AM)* extends to over 200 single malts. Sit in a big leather armchair and gaze out over Trafalgar Square.

The scene is wild at **Bar Rumba (72)** *(36 Shaftesbury Ave., 020-7287-6933, www.barrumbadisco.co.uk; call for hours)*, a club rocking with hard house, Latin, and garage. Cool cocktail bar in the evening, wild queen scene at night, the **Shadow Lounge (75)** *(5 Brewer St., 020-7317-9270, www.theshadowlounge.co.uk; hours: M–Sa 10PM–3AM)* is a slick, stylish gay nightclub.

WHERE TO SHOP

A stop at **Liberty (44)** *(210-220 Regent St., 020-7734-1234, www.liberty.co.uk; hours: M–Sa 10AM–8PM, Su 12PM–6PM)* is de rigueur when in London. The building itself is fabulous *(see page 41)*. Liberty prints made it famous, but it also sells creative original work by jewelers, potters, furniture makers, and textile designers. **A Bathing Ape (76)** *(4 Upper James St., 020-7434-2541, www.bape.com; hours: M–F 11AM–7PM, Sa 11AM–6:30PM, Su 2PM–5PM)* streetwear has become the rage; this is the Japanese brand's only European store. Shops in **Carnaby Street (45)** *(www.carnaby.co.uk)*, **Kingly Court**, and **Fouberts Place** are dominated by up-and-coming young designers. **Newburgh Street (77)** *(www.carnaby.co.uk/catergories/newburgh-quarter)* features street chic in shops like **Jess James**, **Cinch**, **The Dispensary**, and **Carhartt**.

Broadwick Street (46) is typical of the edgier side of British fashion. City camouflage is the trademark of **Maharishi (78)** *(2-3 Great Pulteney St., 020-7287-0388, www.emaharishi.com; hours: M–Sa 11AM–7PM)*. Erotic, humorous, and terribly trendy, **Agent Provocateur (80)** *(6 Broadwick St., 020-7439-0229, www.agentprovocateur.com; hours: M–Sa 11AM–7PM, Th till 8PM, Su 12PM–5PM)* is an expensive, incredibly successful lingerie shop known for its sensuality and glamour. The salespeople wear stilettos, lace stockings, and bustiers

designed by Vivienne Westwood, whose son and daughter-in-law are the owners.

The **Berwick Street Market (81)** is lined with fruit and veggie stands and plenty of indie record stores. If you prefer whisky to artichokes, the **Vintage House (82)** *(42 Old Compton St., 020-7437-5112, www.sohowhisky.com; hours: M–F 9AM–11PM, Sa 9:30AM–11PM, Su 12PM–10PM)* carries malts from every region, as well as other liquor, wines, and cigars.

Charing Cross Road boasts many of London's best bookstores. The famous **Foyles (83)** *(113-119 Charing Cross Rd., 020-7437-5660, www.foyles.co.uk; hours: M–Sa 9:30AM–9PM, Su 11:30AM–6PM)* has incorporated **Silver Moon** women's bookshop and **Ray Jazz**, which organizes music events; other events include book signings and readings. **Blackwell (84)** *(100 Charing Cross Rd., 020-7292-5100, http://bookshop.blackwell.co.uk; hours: M–Sa 9:30AM–8PM, Su 12PM–6PM)* sells a large selection of professional and academic books, as well as general interest. **Henry Pordes Books (85)** *(58-60 Charing Cross Rd., 020-7836-9031, www.henrypordesbooks.com; hours: M–Sa 10AM–7PM, Su 1PM–6PM)* specializes in arts and humanities.

WHERE TO STAY

Hazlitt's (86) *(££-££££)* *(6 Frith St., Soho Sq., 020-7434-1771, www.hazlittshotel.com)* has been a favorite of intel-lectuals, writers, and journalists. Formed from three

Georgian town houses, it is a charm-ing hotel full of antique furniture and paintings—a Merchant Ivory experi-ence. The other end of the chic spec-trum is the **Soho Hotel (87)** *(£££-££££) (4 Richmond Mews, 020-7559-3000, www.sohohotel.com)*—trendy, mod-ern, brightly colored, full of modern artworks, yet supremely comfortable. Hip Londoners stay there for the weekend.

The Trafalgar (88) *(£££) (Trafalgar Sq., 2 Spring Gdns., 020-7870-2900, www.thetrafalgar.com)*, a Hilton hotel, is fun for the young and not technologically challenged. Singers, musicians, or a DJ provide continuous music in the lobby and lounge. The minimalist rooms are offset by eclectically Baroque or street-arty details, and the blue and pink elevators are named Harry and Sally!

The Thistle chain offers clean, average rooms: **Thistle Piccadilly (89)** *(££-£££) (Coventry St., 0871-376-9031, www.thistlehotels.com)* and **The Royal Trafalgar (90)** *(££-£££) (Whitcomb St., Trafalgar Sq., 0871-376-9037, www.thistlehotels.com)*. Cash depleted? **Piccadilly Backpackers (91)** *(£) (12 Sherwood St., 020-7434-9009, www.piccadillybackpackers.com)* is a hostel with very inexpensive single rooms, doubles, and dorms.

⊖ *Covent Garden, Leicester Square, Charing Cross,
Embankment, Temple*

• SNAPSHOT •

In 1635 architect Inigo Jones transformed
★**COVENT GARDEN**—once the grounds of
a convent—into the "in" neighborhood
for 17th-century literary and theatrical connoisseurs.
Henry Fielding, Alexander Pope, James Boswell, and
David Garrick frequented the local theaters and bars
there. Jones's Piazza became the neighborhood's centerpiece. A vegetable market flourished there for three
centuries until 1974, when it moved to South London.
Covent Garden's subsequent gentrification made the
neighborhood hip. Today this beautiful area is a lively
community with a mix of residences, theaters, boutiques, bars, and restaurants. Covent Garden is also
synonymous with the Royal Opera
House, home to a world-renowned
opera and ballet company. This
and other theaters make the quarter, nicknamed "Theatreland,"
popular with the literati.

South of Covent Garden is The Strand, named after the
street that runs through the quarter and connects Trafalgar
Square to the City (London's financial district). It was once

the site of palaces and grand hotels. Although the palaces no longer exist, decorative buildings and the legendary Savoy Hotel conjure images of The Strand's aristocratic past. The art galleries of Somerset House and a number of well-regarded theaters add to The Strand's appeal.

PLACES TO SEE
Landmarks:
Covent Garden Piazza (92) was London's first square, and Inigo Jones designed it to resemble the Italian piazzas he loved, with colonnades and arcades harboring shops and cafés. In 1832 the Central Market, designed by Charles Fowler, went up. An iron and glass canopy linked its three buildings and protected the fruit and vegetable stalls. Today it houses shops of designer clothes, antiques, arts, crafts, books, and housewares. Street entertainers perform under the portico of **St. Paul's Covent Garden (93)** *(Bedford St., 020-7836-5221, www.actorschurch.org; call for hours)*, another Inigo Jones creation. His unorthodox design had the altar at the west end and the grand entrance portico facing east onto the beautiful piazza. This proved unacceptable to the clerics; the altar was placed on the east side, the entrance on the west. So Jones made a fake doorway on the church's east flank, the portico that street performers use as a stage. Connected to the area's many theaters, St. Paul's is known as the Actor's Church. The first scene of George Bernard Shaw's play *Pygmalion* takes place under the east portico. The lovely church courtyard garden is full of flowers and apple trees; famous actors and musicians have been spotted there.

The **Royal Opera House (94)** *(Bow St., box office 020-7304-4000, www.roh.org.uk; public area hours: daily 10AM–3:30PM)*, one of the most prestigious opera houses in the world, is home to the **Royal Opera** and the **Royal Ballet**. The neo-Classical the-ater, with its columns, pediment, portico, and frieze, finds a counterpoint in the stunning iron and glass structure of the adjoining **Vilar Floral Hall**, once the old flower market. Besides performances, the theater gives backstage tours and viewings of the Royal Ballet's classes.

Converted 19th-century warehouses in **Neal Street (95)** and **Neal's Yard (96)**, hoisting equipment still attached to the outer walls, form a trendy area of shops, restaurants, and art galleries. Nearby, at the intersection of seven streets, is the **Seven Dials (97)** *(Monmouth St.)* rotary. Its name comes from the six sundials attached to a Doric column, itself the seventh sundial, in the middle of the rotary. In the 18th century, when a rumor spread through this crime-infested slum that a treasure was buried beneath the column, a greedy mob pulled it down. The pillar standing there today is a replica.

The **London Coliseum (98)** *(St. Martin's Ln., box office 020-7845-9300, www.eno.org; call for hours)* is home to the **English National Opera**. Exuberantly ornate, with its signature cupola, gilded putti, and purple curtains, it is London's largest theater. Nearby is the famous Art Deco

Adelphi Theatre (99) *(Strand, box office: 0844-412-4651, stage door: 020-7836-1166, www.reallyuseful.com/theatres/adelphi-theatre).*

In the glory days, **St. Mary-le-Strand**, **Bush House**, **Savoy Chapel**, and the **Savoy Hotel** were built in high style along The Strand by well-known architects. The gorgeous 18th-century **Somerset House (100)** *(Strand, 020-7845-4600, www.somersethouse.org.uk; hours: daily 10AM–6PM)*, once the site of British naval offices, now houses art galleries, the incredible Courtauld collection, The Admiralty restaurant, and the Riverside Terrace Café.

Along the Thames River, the **Victoria Embankment Gardens (101)** comprise a beautiful tended park on the site where the Duke of York's home once stood. In summer there are free concerts in the gardens. By the river's edge is **Cleopatra's Needle (102)**, an Egyptian obelisk dating from around 1500 B.C. A gift to Britain in 1819 from the Viceroy of Egypt, Mohammed Ali, its hieroglyphics commemorate ancient Egyptian pharaohs. In the base of the obelisk, a Victorian time capsule contains objects from that era, including newspapers, a train schedule, and photos of 12 Victorian women.

Arts & Entertainment:

London's Transport Museum (103) *(39 Wellington St., entrance on Covent Garden Piazza, 020-7379-6344, 020-7565-7298, www.ltmuseum.co.uk; hours: Sa–Th 10AM–6PM, F 11AM–6PM)* presents a social history of

London's evolution through city transportation, including 20th-century commercial art and London Transport posters (by prominent artists of the 1920s and 1930s). Interactive exhibits let kids sit in the driver's seat of a London bus or tube train.

The many galleries of **Somerset House (100)** *(see page 54)* showcase masterpieces of Western art. The **Courtauld Institute of Art Gallery** displays Old Masters and Renaissance paintings and has a very impressive collection of Impressionists and Post-Impressionists. The **Gilbert Collection** of European gold and silver includes enameled portrait miniatures, Italian pietra dura mosaics, and European silverware. The **Hermitage Rooms** display exhibitions of works from the State Hermitage Museum in St. Petersburg.

The **Donmar Warehouse (104)** *(41 Earlham St., Seven Dials, box office: 0844-871-7624, www.donmarwarehouse. com; call for showtimes)* consistently mounts top-notch theatrical productions, both new and classic. Contemporary playwrights whose work has been staged there recently include Tom Stoppard, Neil LaBute, and Mark Ravenhill. The **Novello Theatre (105)** *(Aldwych, 0844-482-5170, www.delfontmackintosh.co.uk; call for showtimes)* mounts musicals. The **Royal Opera** and the **Royal Ballet** perform at the **Royal Opera House (94)**

(see page 53), with the performances' music piped outside to the Piazza.

The **English National Opera** can be seen at the **London Coliseum (98)** *(see page 53)*. Free summer concerts are held at **Victoria Embankment Gardens (101)** *(see page 54)*.

PLACES TO EAT & DRINK
Where to Eat:

Connoisseurs claim **J. Sheekey (106) (££–£££)** *(28-32 St. Martin's Ct., 020-7240-2565, www.caprice-holdings. co.uk; hours: M–Sa 12PM–3PM, 5:30PM–12AM, Su 12PM–3:30PM, 6PM–11PM)* has the best, freshest seafood in London. The decor is plain but the appeal is obvious: this is a hit with the area's theater directors, actors, and producers. Under the same management, ultra-glam **The Ivy (107) (££–££££)** *(1 West St., 020-7836-4751, www. caprice-holdings.co.uk; hours: M–Sa 12PM–11:30PM, Su 12PM–10:30PM)* is where *le tout* theater scene goes, but you might have to reserve weeks ahead. It's famous, friendly, and crowded, and has excellent Modern British and Continental cuisine.

The **Savoy Grill (108) (££–££££)** *(Savoy Hotel, The Strand, 020-7592-1600, www.gordonramsay.com/thesavoygrill, www.fairmont.com/savoy-london; hours: M–Sa 12PM–3PM, 5:30PM–11PM, Su 12PM–4PM, 6PM–10:30PM)* is as suave as its name suggests—you almost expect Cary Grant to pop out from behind a fern and order Châteaubriand, Scottish lobster, or king prawn tortellini. The exalted have dined at **Rules (109) (££–££££)** *(35 Maiden Ln., 020-7836-5314, www.rules.co.uk; hours: M–Sa 12PM–11:30PM, Su 12PM–10:30PM)* ever since Thomas Rule opened the place in 1798. Edward VII,

Charles Dickens, H. G. Wells, and Graham Greene are among those who crossed its threshold more than once. The Edwardian gentlemen's club atmosphere persists, down to the British meat and game.

In lovely Somerset House, **Tom's Kitchen (110) (£-£££)** *(Somerset House, The Strand, 020-7845-4646, www. somersethouse.org.uk; hours: M–F 12PM–3PM, 6PM–10PM, Sa 10AM–4PM, 6PM–10PM, Su 10AM–4PM)* serves classics from burgers and steaks to shepherd's pie and braised oxtail in a casual setting. The courtyard, with 55 fountains, turns into an outdoor ice rink in winter. **Tom's Terrace (111) (£-££)** *(Somerset House, The Strand, 020-7845-4600, www.somersethouse.org.uk; call for hours)* offers al fresco dining or drinks, spring to fall. For a light meal or quick bite, try **The Courtauld Gallery Café (£)** *(020-7848-2527)* at Somerset House.

Bars & Nightlife:
Everywhere you turn in Covent Garden, there are lively bars and clubs. The café of the London Poetry Society, **Poetry Café (112)** *(22 Betterton St., 020-7420-9888, www.poetrysociety.org.uk; hours: M–F 12PM–11PM, Sa 7PM–11PM)*, holds poetry readings, workshops, and music. Tuesday is open-mike night; Saturday, poetry and jazz. The underground **Gordon's Wine Bar (113)** *(47 Villiers St., 020-7930-1408, www.gordonswinebar. com; hours: M–Sa 11AM–11PM, Su 12PM–10PM)*, once a 14th-century port and sherry warehouse, is the real

thing—scruffy and atmospheric with a great selection of wines.

The **Lamb and Flag (114)** *(33 Rose St., 020-7497-9504, www.lambandflagcoventgarden.co.uk; hours: M–Sa 11AM–11PM, Su 12PM–10:30PM, Su jazz 8PM–10:15PM)*, an authentic old Covent Garden pub, has existed since the 16th century. Cocktail lounge and nightclub merge in the dramatic, exotic decor of **Jewel (73)** *(29-30 Maiden Ln., 020-7845-9980, www.jewelbar.com; hours: M–Tu 5PM–12:30AM, W–Sa 5PM–1AM)*. Singer-songwriters headline at **12 Bar Club (115)** *(22-23 Denmark Pl., 020-7240-2120, box office: 020-7240-2622, www.12barclub.com; hours: bar, M–F 11AM–7PM, Sa 12PM–7PM; club, M–Sa 7PM–3AM, Su 7PM–12:30AM)*, a tiny, very cool club. The **Lobby Bar (116)** *(1 Aldwych, 020-7300-1070, www.onealdwych.com; hours: M–F 8AM–12AM, Sa 9AM–12AM, Su 9AM–10:30PM)* at the hotel One Aldwych is an "in" spot, especially for late afternoon cocktails. Legendary **Heaven (117)** *(The Arches, Villiers St., 020-7930-2020, www.heaven-live.co.uk; call for hours)* is one of London's hottest gay clubs.

WHERE TO SHOP

In an area where Stringfellows, the famed lap-dancing club, mingles with the London Coliseum and the Royal Opera House, the range of shops is also vast. One of London's largest shopping areas is **Seven Dials (97)** *(see page 53)*, with quirky shops and designer boutiques mixed in with chain stores. Shoe shops in **Neal Street (95)** offer the gamut of footwear, from sneakers to stilettos. Stroll along Monmouth Street (118) and **Upper St. Martin's Lane** and check out the plethora of interesting shops.  **Coco de Mer** *(23 Monmouth St., 020-7836-8882, www.coco-de-mer.com; hours: M–W, F–Sa 11AM–7PM, Th 11AM–8PM, Su 12PM–6PM)*, founded by Sam Roddick, daughter of Body Shop's Anita Roddick, sells fashion lingerie and erotica. **Dress Circle** *(57-59 Monmouth St., 020-7240-2227, www.dresscircle.co.uk; hours: M–Sa 10AM–6:30PM)* is a bookshop known for recordings of musicals.

Thomas Neal's (119) *(Earlham St.)* is an upscale shopping center while **Neal's Yard (96)** is a vegetarian heaven, abundant in aromatherapy products, homeopathic remedies, creams, lotions, potions, and organic foods.

The vintage clothing at Rokit (120) *(42 Shelton St., 020-7836-6547, www.rokit.co.uk; hours: M–Sa 10AM–7PM, Su 11AM–6PM)* is a big draw, while Rokit's own label is a new phenomenon. Cobblestoned and closed to traffic, **Floral Street** is true-blue British. Here you'll find the first Paul Smith (121) *(40-44 Floral St., 020-7379-7133, www.paulsmith.co.uk; hours: M–W 10:30AM–6:30PM, Th, F 10:30AM–7PM, Sa 10AM–7PM, Su 12:30PM–5:30PM)*

shop. McClintock Eyewear (123) *(29 Floral St., 020-7240-5055, www.mcclintock-eyewear.co.uk; hours: M–Sa 11AM–7PM, Su 12PM–5PM)*, the eyewear designer, has expanded the collection from the family's traditional styles, sported by Michael Caine in his early films, to more updated designs. End your spree with some pampering at The Sanctuary (124) *(12 Floral St., reservations 0845-521-4567, 020-7420-5103, www.thesanctuary.co.uk; hours: M–F 9:30AM–6PM, Sa–Su 9:30AM–8PM)*, a famous women's spa.

WHERE TO STAY

Stunningly beautiful and divinely luxurious, One Aldwych (125) (£££-££££) *(1 Aldwych, 020-7300-1000, www.onealdwych.com)* is a labor of love and talent concocted by financier-connoisseur Gordon Campbell Gray and interior designer Mary Fox Linton. Triangular lobby, contemporary art, high-design elevators, fabulous pool—the place is amazing. Covent Garden Hotel (126) (££££) *(10 Monmouth St., 020-7806-1000, www.coventgardenhotel.co.uk)* is the kind of hideaway that movie stars might go to for a real rest, comfort, and great service.

The **St. Martin's Lane (127)** (£££-££££) *(45 St. Martin's Ln., 020-7300-5500, www.stmartinslane.com)*, designed by Philippe Starck, is drama in light and color; though the rooms are not very big, the hotel is interesting and popular. *Grande dame* of London's hotels, **The Savoy (128)** (£££-££££) *(The Strand, 020-7836-4343, www.savoy2009.com)* harks back to the days of Victorian refinement. It opened in 1889 and has just undergone a £100 million restoration. Its luxury is still legendary, while its lobby is listed as an extraordinary Art Deco achievement.

London is a roost for every bird.
—*Benjamin Disraeli*

chapter 2

ST. JAMES'S

WESTMINSTER

ST. JAMES'S WESTMINSTER

Places to See:

1. St. James's Church
2. St. James's Square
3. Pall Mall
4. Marlborough House
5. Queen's Chapel
6. The Mall
7. Admiralty Arch
8. St. James's Park
9. St. James's Palace
10. Clarence House
11. Spencer House
12. Green Park
13. BUCKINGHAM PALACE ★
14. Queen's Gallery
15. Royal Mews
16. Apsley House: The Wellington Museum
17. ICA–Institute of Contemporary Arts
35. HOUSES OF PARLIAMENT ★
    Westminster Hall
    Big Ben
36. Jewel Tower
37. WESTMINSTER ABBEY ★
38. St. Margaret's Church
39. Downing Street
40. Banqueting House
41. Horse Guards Parade
42. Westminster Cathedral
43. TATE BRITAIN ★
44. Churchill War Rooms
45. Guards Museum
46. St. John's, Smith Square

Places to Eat & Drink:

18. Le Caprice
19. The Wolseley
20. The Avenue
21. Wiltons
22. Fortnum's Fountain
23. The Diamond Jubilee Tea Salon
24. Golden Lion
25. The Red Lion
47. Cinnamon Club
48. Quirinale
49. Shepherd's
50. Rex Whistler Restaurant
51. The Albert
52. Red Lion
53. Westminster Arms
54. Sanctuary House Pub

★ *Top Pick*

Where to Shop:

26. Fortnum & Mason
27. Jermyn Street:
    Hilditch & Key
    Harvie & Hudson
    Dunhill
    John Lobb
28. St. James's Street:
    D.R. Harris & Co. Ltd.
    Berry Bros & Rudd
29. Royal Opera Arcade
30. Prince's Arcade
31. Piccadilly Arcade
55. Blewcoat School

Where to Stay:

32. Sofitel Saint James
34. The Stafford
56. Sanctuary House Hotel
57. DoubleTree by
    Hilton Hotel Westminster
58. Grange Rochester Hotel

ST. JAMES'S

⊖ *Green Park, Hyde Park Corner, Piccadilly Circus, Charing Cross*

● SNAPSHOT ●

Dignified, exclusive St. James's is a quiet, wealthy neighborhood of private gentlemen's clubs, old shops that have catered to the royals for centuries, and residences of the nobility. It is home to St. James's Palace, the official residence of the monarch (the Court of St. James), as well as Buckingham Palace, the actual residence and offices of the Queen. Shops in St. James's cater mostly to traditional, distinctly masculine tastes. Charming old pubs nestle in the streets off Piccadilly, the large avenue that got its name from the stiff collars, or "pickadills," that 17th-century fops wore.

Henry VIII built St. James's Palace on the site of an 11th-century hospital dedicated to St. James the Less, Bishop of Jerusalem. Much later, Henry Jermyn, Earl of St. Albans, developed the district into a suburb for the nobility. Fashionable homes were eventually turned into clubs for wealthy men; some were infamous as gambling places. Many clubs still remain, but the area has been infiltrated by banks and real estate concerns. Stores providing custom-made shirts, hats,

shoes, and boots continue to thrive here, along with jewelers, antiques and fine arts dealers, and auction houses, among others.

PLACES TO SEE
Landmarks:

Designed in 1684 by Sir Christopher Wren, a leading architect in London's restoration after the Great Fire of 1666, **St. James's Church (1)** *(197 Piccadilly, 020-7734-4511, www.st-james-piccadilly.org; call for hours)* is fairly plain, except for the superb altar screen and marble font by 17th-century carver Grinling Gibbons. Classical concerts and a churchyard market make this a popular spot.

St. James's Square (2), one of London's oldest, dates from 1670. Private homes of noblemen once encircled it, replaced by 18th- and 19th-century buildings. The World War II headquarters of Generals Eisenhower and de Gaulle were on the square, while the **London Library**, founded by historian Thomas Carlyle in 1841, lies in the northwest corner. A block away, gentlemen's clubs line the **Pall Mall (3)**. They are examples of the work of some of Britain's outstanding architects, including John Nash *(No. 116)*, Decimus Burton *(No. 107)*, and Sir Charles Barry *(Nos. 104 and 106)*, who designed the Houses of Parliament. **Pall Mall (3)** was a pitching ground for the game *palle-maille*, a hybrid of croquet and golf. **Marlborough House (4)** *(Pall Mall, 020-7747-6500/6491, www.thecommonwealth.org/Internal/34467)*, another Wren creation, was used by the Royal Family during the 19th century—notably by the Prince and Princess of Wales until he became Edward VII in

1901. **Queen's Chapel (5)** *(Marlborough Rd.; hours: open Easter–July for Sun. services, 8:30AM & 11:30AM)*, designed by Inigo Jones in the 1620s, was the first Classical church built in England.

The Mall (6), the processional route created for Queen Victoria, extends from the Victoria Monument in front of Buckingham Palace to Trafalgar Square. At Trafalgar it goes under the **Admiralty Arch (7)** with traffic passing through the two side gates; the central gate opens only for royal processions. South of **The Mall (6)** is exquisite **St. James's Park (8)** *(www.royalparks.org.uk; hours: daily 5AM–12AM)*, beautifully designed with walkways, exuberant flowerbeds, a lake-sanctuary for wildfowl, and lovely ornamental details. Once the royal hunting grounds of Henry VIII, it became a 17th-century pedestrian park under Charles II; its present-day beautiful design is the early 19th-century work of John Nash. The pelicans (of local  celebrity fame) that make the park their home are fed 12 pounds of fish at the lake every day between 2:30PM and 3PM.

St. James's Palace (9) *(Pall Mall, not open to public)*, an important historic site built in the 16th century, is the official residence of the sovereign, although the actual residence is Buckingham Palace. Next door is Prince Charles's home, **Clarence House (10)** *(Stable Yard, 020-7766-7324, www.royalcollection.org.uk; hours: Aug M–F 10AM–4PM, Sa–Su 10AM–5:30PM, guided tours only,* *reserve in advance).* **Spencer House (11)** *(27 St. James's Pl., 020-7514-1958, www.spencerhouse.co.uk; hours: Su 10:30AM–4:45PM, closed Jan & Aug, guided tour only, reserve in advance)*, the opulent Palladian mansion, was built for the first Earl of Spencer, an ancestor of Princess Diana. Now mainly a venue for corporate entertainment, the mansion has limited public access.

West of **St. James's Palace (9)** is **Green Park (12)** *(www. royalparks.org.uk)*. Like **St. James's Park (8)**, this public park was once part of Henry VIII's hunting grounds. It surrounds ★**BUCKINGHAM PALACE (13)** *(020-7766-7300, www.royal collection.org.uk, www.royal.gov.uk; tickets by phone or from Ticket Office at Visitor Entrance, Buckingham Palace Rd.; July–Sep 9:15AM–5PM)*, home of the British monarchy since 1837. It was built in 1703 as a town house for the Duke of Buckingham. John Nash turned it into a grand palace for George IV. The **State Rooms** are open to the public in August *(9:30AM–7PM)*, and September *(9:30AM–6:30PM)*, when the Queen is at **Balmoral**, her Scottish castle. They contain cherished works of art from masters such as Rembrandt, Rubens, and Vermeer, as well as refined English and French furniture. When the Queen is in residence at **Buckingham Palace (13)**, the Royal Standard (her royal flag) flies from atop the front entrance. About 300 people work at the 775-room palace, with staff housed in the palace and the Royal Mews. Don't miss the famous **Changing of the Guards**, which takes place in the palace forecourt *(see also page 20)*.

TOP PICK!

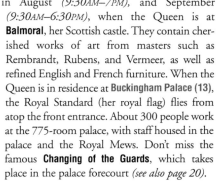

Arts & Entertainment:

The **Queen's Gallery (14)** *(Buckingham Palace Rd., 020-7766-7324, www.royalcollection.org.uk; hours: daily 10AM–5:30PM)* contains the Queen's art collection, one of the most valuable in the world. At the **Royal Mews (15)** *(Buckingham Palace Rd., 020-7766-7324, www.royalcollection.org.uk; hours:* 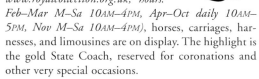 *Feb–Mar M–Sa 10AM–4PM, Apr–Oct daily 10AM–5PM, Nov M–Sa 10AM–4PM)*, horses, carriages, harnesses, and limousines are on display. The highlight is the gold State Coach, reserved for coronations and other very special occasions.

Apsley House: The Wellington Museum (16) *(149 Piccadilly, Hyde Park Corner, 020-7499-5676, www.english-heritage.org.uk; hours: Apr–Oct W–Su 11AM–5PM, Nov–Mar Sa–Su 10AM–4PM)* became the home of the Duke of Wellington, the military genius who defeated Napoleon at Waterloo in 1815 and twice served as Prime Minister. His fine collection of art and personal memorabilia are on display. The Duke's humor is evident in the Canova statue of Napoleon, his arch-enemy, sporting only a fig leaf. **Wellington Arch**, in front of Apsley House, holds exhibitions in its interior rooms; from its platform the views of London are breathtaking.

The Nash House is home to London's foremost institution of modern and contemporary art, the **ICA–Institute of Contemporary Arts (17)** *(12 Carlton House Terrace, The Mall, 020-7930-0493, box office 020-7930-3647,* *www.ica.org.uk; hours: Tu–Su 11AM–11PM, Galleries Tu–Su 11AM–6PM, Th til 9PM).* Founded by a group of artists, poets, and writers in 1947, it has exhibited works by artists who have challenged the traditional, academic approach and is a forum for some of the most progressive art today. International films are also screened here.

PLACES TO EAT & DRINK
Where to Eat:

Charming and elegant, **Le Caprice (18) (££–£££)** *(Arlington House, Arlington St., 020-7629-2239,*

www.caprice-holdings.co.uk; hours: M–F 12PM–12AM, Sa 11:30AM–4PM, 5:30PM–12AM, Su 11:30AM–5PM, 5:30PM–11PM) is a legend of Modern British cuisine and a huge draw for celebrities. **The Wolseley (19) (££–££££)** *(160 Piccadilly, 020-7499-6996, www.thewolseley.com; hours: M–F 7AM–12AM, Sa 8AM–12AM, Su 8AM–11PM)* is sophisticated and elegant; its fine menu, dramatic interior, and elegant service keep the famous and otherwise loyal customers. Cool is the word for **The Avenue (20) (££–£££)** *(7-9 St. James's St., 020-7321-2111, www.avenue-restaurant.co.uk; hours: M–F 12PM–3PM, 5:45PM–11PM, Sa 5:45PM–11PM)*, with its minimalist interior and long, glass-topped bar, where the chic and sassy gather for the excellent Modern British-French fare. The grand, traditional, and very formal ambience of **Wiltons (21) (££–££££)** *(55 Jermyn St., 020-7629-9955, www.wiltons.co.uk; hours: M–F*

12PM–2:30PM, 5:30PM–10:30PM) makes it old-school British, though the menu is a mix of flamboyant French and staid British. Seafood is the specialty, but the lobster, crab, and truffle omelette or braised ox tongue in Madeira with mashed potatoes are remarkable.

Unchanged since 1950, **Fortnum's Fountain (22) (£-£££)** *(Fortnum & Mason, ground floor, 181 Piccadilly, 020-7734-8040, reservations 0845-602-5694, www.fortnumand mason.com; hours: M–F 7AM–9PM, Sa 8AM–9PM, Su 8AM–6PM)* is a favorite café  in the famous epicurean store. Traditional and healthy dishes range from Welsh rarebit to caviar and champagne. Don't forget the ice cream sundae. Or do a more formal lunch or afternoon tea **(£££)** upstairs at **The Diamond Jubilee Tea Salon (23) (£-££)** *(Fortnum & Mason, 4th Floor, 181 Piccadilly, 020-7734-8040, reservations 0845-602-5694, www.fortnumandmason.com; hours: M–Sa 12PM–9PM, Su 12PM–8PM).*

Bars & Nightlife:
The **Golden Lion (24)** *(25 King St., 020-7925-0007; hours: M–F 11AM–11PM, Sa 12PM–8PM)* dates from the early-18th century. Black marble columns and the mahogany and glass interior make it an unusual pub. Equally upscale, **The Red Lion (25)** *(23 Crown Passage, off King St., 020-7930-4141; hours: M–Sa 11:30AM–11PM)* carries its Victorian charm with dignity.

WHERE TO SHOP

Fortnum & Mason (26) *(181 Piccadilly, 020-7734-8040, www.fortnumandmason.com; hours: M–Sa 10AM–8PM, Su 12PM–6PM)* began in 1707 as a grocery store founded by William Fortnum, a footman to Queen Anne, and Hugh Mason, a St. James's shopkeeper. Its fine quality foods became the rage and have remained so. The rest of the store has wonderful finds, all sorts of interesting objects, and chic clothing. Architecturally, the interior is fantastic—pre-war elegance, with wood staircases and shelving and beautifully designed doors. The ground-floor food hall, with its chandeliers and marbled pillars, is delightfully flamboyant.

Jermyn Street (27) is known for its bespoke men's shirts and boots. Many of their makers hold royal warrants, an honor for supplying high-quality goods to members of the Royal Family. One of the oldest shirtmakers is **Hilditch & Key** *(37 Jermyn St., 020-7734-4707, www.hilditchandkey.co.uk)*, which includes a women's section. **Harvie & Hudson** *(97 Jermyn St., 020-7839-3578, www.harvieandhudson.com; hours: M–Sa 9:30AM–6PM, Su 11AM–4PM)*, with its beautiful Victorian façade, caters to traditional men's tastes, while the elegance of **Dunhill** *(48 Jermyn St., 020-7290-8609, www.dunhill.com)* has a more modern allure. **John Lobb** *(88 Jermyn St., 020-7930-8089, www.johnlobbltd.co.uk; also at 9 St. James's St., 020-7930-3664; hours: M–F 9AM–5:30PM, Sa 9AM–4:30PM)* custom-makes shoes for the Queen, the Duke of

Edinburgh, and Prince Charles. Each piece is numbered and comes in fine materials, from buckskin to crocodile to ostrich, and in all imaginable colors. They also sell ready-to-wear men's shoes and boots.

At the end of **Jermyn Street (27)**, stroll down charming **St. James's Street (28)**. Many of the shops date from Victorian and Edwardian times. The wonderfully old-fashioned chemist's shop (apothecary) **D. R. Harris & Co. Ltd.** *(29 St. James's St., 020-7930-3915, www.drharris. co.uk; hours: M–F 8:30AM–6PM, Sa 9:30AM–5PM)* has all sorts of brushes, razors, and bath and beauty products, including its own line: two favorites are Crystal Eye Gel and Bay Rum Aftershave. The gorgeous 18th-century shop front of **Berry Bros & Rudd** *(3 St. James's St., 0800-280-2440, www.bbr.com; hours: M–F 9AM–6PM, Sa 10AM–5PM)* is the façade of one of the oldest wine merchants in the world. Founded in 1698, they've been supplying the Royal Family with fine vintages since 1760.

The first of the covered shopping arcades, **Royal Opera Arcade (29)** *(between Charles II St. and Pall Mall, just behind Haymarket, www.royaloperaarcade.com; hours: M–Sa 8AM–7:30PM)* was built in 1818. Its vaulted ceilings, lovely lanterns, and charming store windows are as beautiful for strolling as for shopping. Menswear stores are the theme in **Prince's Arcade (30)** *(off Piccadilly, www.princesarcade.co.uk; hours: M–Sa 8AM–7PM, Su 10AM–5PM)* and **Piccadilly Arcade (31)** *(off Piccadilly,*

www.piccadilly-arcade.com), the early-19th-century covered passages off Jermyn Street. A lively market in the churchyard of **St. James's Church (1)** *(www. piccadilly-market.co.uk, also see page 66)* sells antiques *(Tu 10AM–6PM)* and arts and crafts *(W–Sa 10AM–6PM)*.

WHERE TO STAY

There is only distinctiveness, not bargains, in St. James's. **Sofitel Saint James (32)** *(££££) (6 Waterloo Place, 020-7747-2200, www.sofitelstjames.com)* is located in what was once an elegant bank in John Nash's Regent Street style. The interior, by French designer Pierre-Yves Rochon, combines British and French accents, with old English furniture, wallpaper with a clock motif, and fabrics in subtle tones. **The Stafford (34)** *(£££-££££) (16–18 St. James's Pl., 020-7493-0111, www.thestaffordhotel. co.uk)*, serene and genteel, exudes British charm.

WESTMINSTER

Charing Cross, Embankment, Westminster, St. James's Park, Victoria, Pimlico

• SNAPSHOT •

The power and pageantry of British royal, political, and religious history comprise the character and the daily activities of Westminster. Carriages of royal and state dignitaries proceed through the streets of the quarter during state visits, and Queen Elizabeth presides over the State opening of Parliament. Two of the most important British institutions are located here: the Palace of Westminster, where the two Houses of Parliament sit; and Westminster Abbey, where the Coronation ceremony, royal weddings, and other exceptional royal and state events take place.

In 1042 Edward the Confessor became king, and a few years later began his plan to enlarge a small church that stood near the swampy Thames, making it England's largest abbey. A minster is an abbey church, so the name of both the church and the area means "the minster in the west." After the Norman Conquest in 1066, William I was the first monarch to be crowned in Westminster Abbey. Since then all but two British sovereigns (Edward V and Edward VIII) were coronated there. Edward the Confessor also built the Palace of Westminster next door. Over the centuries the royal palace was destroyed by fires; after the last devastating one in 1834, Charles Barry set about designing a new plan for what today are the Houses of Parliament.

By day Westminster is alive with the business of running government, but at night it closes shop and becomes quite deserted. All vestiges of pomp and circumstance disappear, with only the monuments to England's heroes casting long shadows on the avenues.

PLACES TO SEE
Landmarks:

When Henry VIII abandoned the original Palace of Westminster in 1532, it was turned over to Parliament, which, until then, had met in the choir pews of St. Stephen's Chapel. Members sat facing each other from opposite sides, and the custom has continued to this day with the Government sitting on the left, the Opposition on the right, and the Speaker seated between them. The neo-Gothic splendor of today's ★HOUSES OF PARLIAMENT (35) *(Parliament Sq., 020-7219-3000; tours info: 0844-847-1672, www.parliament.uk; overseas visitors may only tour on Sa and during "Summer Opening": Sa 9:15AM–4:30PM, Aug–Sep call for hours; Parliamentary sessions are open to the public; House of Commons info: 020-7219-4272; House of Lords info: 020-7219-3107)* exudes the extravagance and confidence of the Victorian era in which they were built. The

TOP PICK!

House of Lords is made up of peers, that is, members of the nobility, many of whom got their titles through service to their country. The House of Commons is an elected body with Members of Parliament (MPs) from a variety of political parties. Whichever gets the most MPs in the elections forms the Government, with that party's leader as Prime Minister. The Opposition includes the MPs from all the other parties. You can attend sessions of either House in the Visitors' Galleries. In summer, when Parliament is not in session, other chambers are open to the public. The superb 11th-century **Westminster Hall** *(Houses of Parliament)* is one of two surviving structures of the medieval Palace of Westminster. In the past century monarchs and Winston Churchill have lain in state there. **Big Ben** *(Houses of Parliament)* is at the end of the Houses of Parliament. Though most people think it's the famous four-sided clock in the tall tower, the name actually belongs to the enormous 13-ton bell inside that rings on the hour. The name  memorializes Sir Benjamin Hall, chief commissioner of works in 1858 when Big Ben was hung. **Jewel Tower (36)** *(Abingdon St., 020-7222-2219, www.english-heritage.org.uk; hours: Apr–Oct daily 10AM–5PM, Nov–Mar Sa–Su 10AM–4PM)* joins Westminster Hall as the other remaining structure of the original medieval Palace. It was built in 1365 to store Edward III's treasures.

TOP PICK!

Glorious ★**WESTMINSTER ABBEY (37)** *(Broad Sanctuary, 020-7222-5152, tours: 020-7654-4832, www.westminster-abbey.org; hours: M–Sa 9:30AM–3:30PM, Su worship only)* is one of the national treasures of England, emblematic of the nation's history and psyche. It is the tomb of British kings and queens. It houses monuments to great British figures—from statesmen to musicians. Samuel Johnson, Dryden, Browning, and Tennyson are buried there in **Poets' Corner**. A mix of architectural styles has been incorporated into the building. It has typically Gothic flying buttresses and pointed arches. At almost 102 feet, it has the highest Gothic vault in England. English characteristics can be seen in the overall sculptural decorations, particularly the lavishly designed moldings of the main arches. Other highlights include the **Tomb of the Unknown Warrior** (commemorating those lost during World War I) and the **Henry VII Chapel** (also known as **Lady Chapel**), which showcases beautiful fan vaulting.

St. Margaret's Church (38) *(St. Margaret St., 020-7654-4840, www.westminster-abbey.org; hours: M–F 9:30AM–3:30PM, Sa 9:30AM–1:30PM, Su 2PM–4:30PM)*, with its elegant Tudor monuments and exquisite stained-glass windows, is a favorite wedding venue for the non-royal hoi polloi. Winston and Clementine Churchill were married there. The east window was commissioned in 1501 by Ferdinand and Isabella of Spain for the marriage of their daughter Catherine of Aragon to Arthur, Henry VIII's brother. By the time it was completed, Arthur was dead and Catherine engaged to Henry VIII.

North on Whitehall, the **Cenotaph**, built by Sir Edward Lutyens, is a memorial to the dead of World Wars I and II. Nearby, also on Whitehall, stands a **monument to the women of WWII** designed by sculptor John Mills. The bronze monument has work clothes hanging from pegs to represent the many different work roles that seven million women took on during the war. The Speaker of the House who presided over the 2005 unveiling ceremony said, "They quietly took them off at the end of the day, hung them up and let the men take the credit." On famous **Downing Street (39)**, No. 10 is the official residence of the Prime Minister and No. 11 that of the Chancellor of the Exchequer. **Banqueting House (40)** *(Whitehall, 020-3166-6154/5, www.hrp.org.uk; hours: daily 10AM–5PM)* is what remains of the Tudor Whitehall Palace after the fire of 1698. Inigo Jones designed the simple, elegant stone exterior in the Palladian style. In stunning counterpoint, however, the magnificently intricate ceiling inside was painted by Rubens. Commissioned by King Charles I, it glorifies his father, James I. In 1649 a disdainful Oliver Cromwell chose this spot to behead Charles I.

The Household Cavalry performs the daily ceremonial mounting of the Queen's Life Guards for the Changing of the Guards on **Horse Guards Parade (41)** *(Whitehall, 020-7766-7300, www.army.mod.uk)* at 11AM (10AM Su). The dismounting ceremony takes place at 4PM in the Front Yard of House Guards *(see page 20 for more on Changing of*

the Guards). The neo-Byzantine **Westminster Cathedral (42)** *(Ashley Pl., 020-7798-9055, www.westminstercathedral. org.uk; hours: info desk daily 10AM–5PM)* is a Catholic church built in 1903, with the famous Eric Gill sculptures of the Stations of the Cross. Majestic marble columns and mosaics grace the interior; due to lack of funding the domes above the nave were left unadorned.

Arts & Entertainment:

TOP PICK!

After the National Gallery, the ★**TATE BRITAIN (43)** *(Millbank, 020-7887-8888, www.tate.org.uk; hours: daily 10AM–6PM)* contains London's second most important collection of art, spanning 500 years from the 16th century to the present. It includes works by Hogarth, Turner, Constable, Whistler, William Blake, Peter Blake, Gainsborough, Reynolds, Bacon, and Moore, among others. Though the **Tate Modern** *(see page 193)* on the South Bank contains most of the collection's contemporary work, the Britain also houses works by Lucian Freud, David Hockney, and Howard Hodgkin. The **Tate-to-Tate Boat Service** crosses the river between the two museums (every 20 min.) and gives you an eyeful of riverside landmarks. The ferry, whose decor was designed by Damien Hirst, also stops at the **London Eye** *(see page 186)*.

Jewel Tower (36) *(see page 77)* is devoted to exhibits on the history of Parliament. During World War II the War Cabinet met in what is now called the **Churchill War Rooms (44)** *(Clive Steps, King Charles St., 020-7930-*

6961, www.iwm.org.uk; hours: daily 9:30AM–6PM). The rooms of this military museum have been preserved as they were when the war ended. In an annex is the **Churchill Museum**. At the **Guards Museum (45)** *(Wellington Barracks, Birdcage Walk, 020-7414-3428/3271, www.theguardsmuseum.com; hours: daily 10AM–4PM)*, the biggest draws are the dioramas and tableaux of battles involving the Guards since the 1642–1648 English Civil War.

There are free recitals every Sunday at 4:45PM at **Westminster Cathedral (42)** *(see page 80)*, which houses one of Europe's finest organs. **St. John's, Smith Square (46)** *(Smith Sq., 020-7222-1061, www.sjss.org.uk; call for showtimes)*, once a Baroque church, is now a concert hall. The Academy of Ancient Music, the Monteverdi Choir, the London Mozart Players, and Polyphony perform there.

PLACES TO EAT & DRINK
Where to Eat:
The **Cinnamon Club (47)** **(££-££££)** *(The Old Westminster Library, 30-32 Great Smith St., 020-7222-2555, www. cinnamonclub.com; hours: M–F 7:30AM–9:30AM, 12PM–2:45PM, 6PM–10:30PM, Sa 12PM–2:45PM, 6PM–10:30PM)* is a magnet for MPs as well as a young, chic crowd. Its food, an innovative take on Indian cuisine, is excellent. **Quirinale (48)** **(££-£££)** *(1 Great Peter St., 020-7222-7080, www.quirinale.co.uk; hours: M–F 12PM–2:30PM, 6PM–10:30PM)* serves great Italian food in an intimate setting. Comfort food—British style—is what you get at reliable

Shepherd's (49) (££-£££) *(Marsham Ct., Marsham St., 020-7834-9552, www.langansrestaurants.co.uk; hours: M–F 12PM–3PM, 6PM–11PM).* The **Rex Whistler Restaurant (50) (££)** *(Tate Britain, Millbank, 020-7887-8825, www.tate.org.uk; call for hours),* minimalist in design, relaxing in atmosphere, offers an excellent Modern British menu.

Bars & Nightlife:

The Albert (51) *(52 Victoria St., 020-7222-5577; hours: M–Sa 10AM–12AM, Su 12PM–10:30PM)* is a charming, atmospheric 19th-century pub packed with happy customers. When it's time for important votes in the House of Commons, a bell rings at the **Red Lion (52)** *(48 Parliament St., 020-7930-5826; hours: M–Sa 10AM–11PM, Su 10AM–9PM)* to tear MPs away from this fabulous etched glass and mahogany bar to do their duty. Other charming, authentic pubs in the area are the **Westminster Arms (53)** *(9 Storey's Gate, 020-7222-8520, www.westminsterarmslondon.co.uk; hours: M–Sa 11AM–11PM, Su 12PM–10:30PM)* and **Sanctuary House Pub (54)** *(33 Tothill St., 020-7799-4044, www.fullershotels.com; hours: M–Sa 8AM–11PM, Su 8AM–10:30PM).*

WHERE TO SHOP

Blewcoat School (55) *(23 Caxton St., 020-7222-2877, www.nationaltrust.org.uk),* an early 18th-century school for educating the poor, belongs to the National Trust, which has a gift shop and information center there. The gift shop at the **Banqueting House (40)** *(see page 79)* features reproductions of the monument's Rubens ceiling.

WHERE TO STAY

Sanctuary House Hotel (56) (£-££) *(33 Tothill St., 020-7799-4044, www.fullershotels.com)* is a refurbished Victorian hotel above a pub, with large, bright rooms, close to the Westminster sights. **DoubleTree by Hilton Hotel Westminster (57)** (££-£££) *(30 John Islip St., 020-7630-1000, doubletree3.hilton.com)* has a minimalist kind of chic. The **Grange Rochester Hotel (58)** (£-££) *(69 Vincent Sq., 020-7828-6611, www.grangehotels.com)*, though a hike from the nearest Tube station, is romantic. Large, beautifully furnished bedrooms have hand-carved rosewood pieces and marble bathrooms.

chapter 3

HYDE PARK & KENSINGTON GARDENS

KNIGHTSBRIDGE, SOUTH KENSINGTON, & BELGRAVIA

CHELSEA

HYDE PARK & KENSINGTON GARDENS
KNIGHTSBRIDGE, SOUTH KENSINGTON, & BELGRAVIA
CHELSEA

Places to See:

1. Speakers' Corner
2. Marble Arch
3. Serpentine
4. Diana, Princess of Wales Memorial Playground
5. KENSINGTON PALACE ★
6. Albert Memorial
7. Serpentine Gallery
11. Oratory of St. Philip Neri
12. Harrods
13. VICTORIA AND ALBERT MUSEUM ★
14. Science Museum
15. Natural History Museum
16. Royal College of Music
17. Royal Albert Hall
18. Royal College of Art
45. Sloane Square
46. King's Road
47. Chelsea Old Church
48. Cheyne Walk
49. Royal Hospital Chelsea
50. Chelsea Physic Garden
51. Royal Court Theatre
52. Carlyle's House
53. National Army Museum

Places to Eat & Drink:

8. Kensington Palace Orangery
19. Marcus Wareing at the Berkeley
20. Outlaw's at the Capital
22. Dinner by Heston Blumenthal
23. Nag's Head
24. Grenadier
25. Bunch of Grapes
26. Blue Bar
27. Bouji's
54. Bibendum Oyster Bar
55. Tom Aikens
56. Rasoi Vineet Bhatia
57. The Builders Arms
58. Big Easy
59. Admiral Codrington
60. Chelsea Potter

★ *Top Pick*

HYDE PARK & KENSINGTON GARDENS

⊖ Hyde Park Corner, Knightsbridge, Marble Arch,
Lancaster Gate, Queensway

• SNAPSHOT •

Sprawling Hyde Park and Kensington Gardens are an oasis of green in central London. Rollerbladers, joggers, boaters, equestrians, bicyclists, and dogwalkers crisscross Hyde Park daily, while at Speaker's Corner anyone can rant or pontificate about their pet theme. The park is also the stage for demonstrations, concerts, and celebrations. Kensington Gardens, to the west, is the formal garden attached to Kensington Palace. Once separate entities, Kensington Gardens and Hyde Park are now smoothly conjoined.

PLACES TO SEE
Landmarks:

In the past, **Hyde Park** *(030-0061-2000, www.royal parks.gov.uk; hours: daily 5AM–12AM)* has been a hunting ground, racetrack, armaments depot, dueling spot, and execution field. **Speakers' Corner (1)** *(near Marble Arch)* was established in 1872 in response to the legalization of freedom of speech and assembly. Anyone can mount their soap box and address the public on the topic of their choice—but can't disturb the peace. Best time is Sunday mornings. **Marble Arch (2)** *(northeast corner, near Marble Arch underground)*, inspired by the Arch of Constantine in Rome, stands beside what was once Tyburn gallows, where public executions took place. The **Serpentine (3)** is the city's oldest boating lake. Within the park, there are also a bird sanctuary and areas for tennis, golf, and bowling. There's also a bandstand, which is a popular meeting place for rollerbladers. Check out *www.londonskaters.com* for events.

Kensington Gardens *(020-7298-2141, www.royalparks.gov.uk; daily 6AM–dusk)*, the grounds of Kensington Palace, features the Round Pond, Long Water (the continuation of the Serpentine), lovely statues, and many beautifully landscaped flowerbeds and borders. The **Diana, Princess of Wales Memorial Playground (4)** *(near Black Lion Gate, Broad Walk, Kensington Gardens, 030-0061-2001, www. royalparks.gov.uk; hours: May–Aug 10AM–7:45PM, Apr & Sep 10AM–6:45PM, Mar & early Oct 10AM–5:45PM, Feb & late Oct 10AM–4:45PM, Nov–Jan 10AM–3:45PM, adults must be accompanied by a child except from 9:30AM–10AM)* is a child's delight, with tree houses, wigwams, a pirate ship, a mermaids' fountain, and plenty of rock formations.

TOP PICK!

For over 300 years a number of monarchs and royals, from William and Mary to Princess Di, have lived in ★**KENSINGTON PALACE (5)** *(info: 0844-482-7777, tickets: 0844-482-7799, www.hrp.org.uk; hours: Mar–Oct daily*

10AM–6PM, Nov–Feb daily 10AM–5PM).
The 18th-century state rooms are open to
the public. The **King's Apartments** display
works of art from the Royal Collection,
including works by William Kent. Some

of the rooms look as they originally did, with lavish decorations. Queen Victoria was christened in 1819 in the
Cupola Room (part of the King's Apartments). The
Queen's Apartments were built as private, intimate rooms
for Queen Mary II. It's doubtful you'd ever find bed
linens and textiles as high quality as those found in her
royal bedroom! Family portraits also hang in the rooms.
To check out fashions of the 18th century, head into the
Royal Ceremonial Dress Collection. In addition to the
dresses, the display contains a tailor's shop, dressing
rooms, and a dressmaker's workroom.

The famous **Albert Memorial (6)** *(South Carriage Drive,
Kensington Gdns., opposite Royal Albert Hall)* is a
grandiose, ornate monument to Queen Victoria's hus-
band, Prince Albert, epitomizing the Victorian aesthetic.

Arts & Entertainment:
The **Serpentine Gallery (7)** *(Kensington Gardens, West
Carriage Drive, near Albert Memorial, 020-7402-6075,
www.serpentinegallery.org; hours: daily 10AM–6PM during
exhibitions)* mounts exciting contemporary art exhibits.
Each summer a world-renowned architect is invited to
create a temporary piece for the gallery's front lawn.
These have included Zaha Hadid, Toyo Ito, and Daniel
Libeskind.

PLACES TO EAT & DRINK
Where to Eat:

A light lunch or afternoon tea at the **Kensington Palace Orangery (8) (£)** *(Kensington Palace, Kensington Gardens, 020-3166-6113, www.hrp.org.uk; hours: Mar–Sep daily 9AM–6PM, Oct–Feb daily 10AM–5PM)* is a delightfully genteel yet relaxed affair in an airy, beautiful setting.

WHERE TO SHOP

Pick up postcards of the royal palace at the Kensington Palace Gift Shop (9) *(Kensington Palace, info: 0844-482-7777; hours: Nov–Feb daily 10AM–5PM, Mar–Oct daily 10AM–6PM)*. It also has an array of specially-designed lace accessories and china. The Family Shop (10) *(Kensington Palace, info: 0844-482-7777)* offers a range of lovely items for children.

For Bars & Nightlife, as well as Hotels, see nearby areas of Knightsbridge, South Kensington & Belgravia.

⊖ *Knightsbridge, Hyde Park Corner, South Kensington*

● SNAPSHOT ●

Legend has it that two knights fought on a bridge of the Westbourne River (later dammed up and turned into the Serpentine); both died and left Knightsbridge as their legacy. These days all anyone battles is the queues at cash registers of this posh quarter's many shops.

While Knightsbridge is a shopper's dream, Belgravia is a wealthy residential area. Besides lovely homes and leafy spots, such as Wilton Crescent and Belgrave Square, it claims a few charming pubs. Farther west, South Kensington encompasses a plethora of museums, academic institutions, and international institutes. The highlight is the Victoria and Albert Museum, whose exciting, cutting-edge exhibitions add verve to a traditional neighborhood.

PLACES TO SEE
Landmarks:

The **Oratory of St. Philip Neri (11)** *(Thurloe Pl., Brompton Rd., 020-7808-0900, www.bromptonoratory.com; call for hours)*, or the Brompton Oratory, is a sumptuous

Catholic church in Italian Baroque style. Ornate mosaics, statues, and ivory-inlaid carved choir stalls are among its many splendors. An altogether different classic is Harrods (12) *(see page 95)*, London's most famous department store. Its dome, olive green awnings, and green-uniformed doormen are hard to miss. At night 11,500 small bulbs outline the store in lights.

Arts & Entertainment:

TOP PICK!

The magnificent ★VICTORIA AND ALBERT MUSEUM (13) *(Cromwell Rd., 020-7942-2000, www.vam.ac.uk; hours: Sa–Th 10AM–5:45PM, F 10AM–10PM)* is the world's largest museum of applied and decorative arts from early Christian times to the present and from all corners of the globe. Don't miss the V&A's British, Glass, South Asia, Fashion, and Sculpture Galleries (or the V&A's Museum Shop). In other words, book a good amount of time for this visit. Renaissance sculpture enthusiasts won't want to miss works by Donatello and Bernini, as well as the prized Michelangelo sculpture, *Slave*. The famous 16th-century Great Bed of Ware showcases the elaborate carvings of English woodworkers. The "great" bed mea-

sures about 12 ft. x 12 ft. and is over 8 ft. high. In addition to the numerous fascinating permanent exhibits, the museum also has a program of changing exhibits on architecture, photography, fashion, and design.

Equally fascinating, the **Science Museum (14)** *(Exhibition Rd., 0870-870-4868, 020-7942-4000, www.science museum.org.uk; hours: daily 10AM–6PM)* covers scientific and technological developments and their impact on daily life. The interactive displays emphasize the magic and science of the process of discovery. Human and animal development is as engrossing at the **Natural History Museum (15)** *(Cromwell Rd., 020-7942-5000, www.nhm.ac.uk; hours: daily 10AM–5:50PM)* as the building itself, a marvel of Victorian architecture. The **Royal College of Music (16)** *(Prince Consort Rd., 020-7591-4300, box office 020-7591-4300, www.rcm.ac.uk; hours: box office M–F 10AM–4PM, call for concert times/museum hours)* holds concerts; its musical instrument museum houses over 800 instruments and accessories *(open Tu–F 2PM–4:30PM)*. The **Royal Albert Hall (17)** *(Kensington Gore, tours and box office: 0845-401-5034, www.royal alberthall.com; call for showtimes and tour times)* is most often the venue for classical music concerts but also other types of performances. Amidst the profusion of Victorian buildings, the glass façade of the **Royal College of Art (18)** *(Kensington Gore, 020-7590-4444, www.rca.ac.uk; call for hours)* seems shocking. Lectures, presentations, and exhibitions are held at the alma mater of David Hockney, Eduardo Paolozzi, and Peter Blake, among others.

PLACES TO EAT & DRINK
Where to Eat:

Reservations are essential at the spectacular **Marcus Wareing at the Berkeley (19)** *(££££) (Berkeley Hotel, Wilton Pl., 020-7235-1200, www.the-berkeley.co.uk;*

hours: *M–Sa noon–2:30PM, 6PM–11PM*). Splurge on the 8-course tasting menu. Exquisite French cuisine is on the plate at **Outlaw's at the Capital (20)** *(££–£££) (The Capital Hotel, 22 Basil St., 020-7591-1202, www.capitalhotel.co.uk; hours: M–Sa noon–2:30PM, 6:30PM–10:30PM)*, a très, très chic establishment, so swathe yourself in silk and jewels. **Dinner by Heston Blumenthal (22)** *(£££–££££) (Mandarin Oriental Hotel, 66 Knightsbridge, 020-7201-3833, www.dinnerbyheston.com, www.mandarinoriental.com/london; hours: daily 12PM–2:30PM, 6:30PM–10:30PM)* has spectacular views of the Royal Park and superb food by internationally acclaimed Chef Heston Blumenthal.

Bars & Nightlife:

The **Nag's Head (23)** *(53 Kinnerton St., 020-7235-1135; M–Sa 11AM–11PM, Su 12PM–10:30PM)*, a charming, tiny pub, boasts an assortment of rare and common ales. The **Grenadier (24)** *(18 Wilton Row, 020-7235-3074; hours: M–Sa 12PM–11PM, Su 12PM–10:30PM)*, a tatty but grand old pub, was once the mess of the Guards officers and said to have been one of Wellington's watering holes. The **Bunch of Grapes (25)** *(207 Brompton Rd., 020-7589-4944; hours: M–Sa 11AM–11PM, Su 12PM–10:30PM)* is a typical Victorian pub: mahogany, glass, and wrought iron are part of its charm. Cool and sleek, the **Blue Bar (26)** *(Berkeley Hotel, Wilton Pl., 020-7235-6000, www.the-berkeley.co.uk; hours: M–Sa 9AM–1AM, Su 9AM–11PM)* serves serious, traditional cocktails to a fashionable clientele. **Bouji's (27)** *(43 Thurloe St., 020-7584-2000, www.boujis.com; hours: Tu–Su 10:30PM–3AM)* is a hot club that has seen Princes William and Harry as well as Britney Spears cross its threshold.

WHERE TO SHOP

Designer boutiques and interesting shops abound in Knightsbridge. Some of the top destinations are **Sloane Street (28)**, **Pont Street (29)**, **Brompton Road (30)**, and **Beauchamp Place (31)**. It is home to two famous department stores. **Harrods (12)** *(87-135 Brompton Rd., 020-7730-1234, www.harrods.com; hours: M–Sa 10AM–8PM, Su 11:30AM–6PM)*

began as a grocery in 1849. In 1919 it sold an airplane; and in 1967, a baby elephant (a gift from the Prince of Albania to Ronald Reagan). **Café Godiva**, the chocolate bar on the second floor, is dreamy: paddles churn large vats of chocolate, which is channeled in brass pipes to the bar where it's on tap! But beware: a small cup of chocolate potion and a chocolate-covered croissant can cost around £12. **Harvey Nichols (32)** *(109–125 Knightsbridge, 020-7235-5000, www.harveynichols.com; hours: M–Sa 10AM–8PM, Su 11:30AM–6PM)* is more modern and eclectic in its range of luxury products.

Fabulous fabrics give an edge to the comfortable fashions at **Egg (33)** *(36 Kinnerton St., 020-7235-9315, www.eggtrading.com; hours: M–Sa 10AM–6PM)*, inspired by work clothes and made in India. Famous fashion eyewear by Cutler & Gross (34) *(16 Knightsbridge Green, 020-7581-2250, www.cutlerandgross.com; hours: M–Sa 9:30AM–7PM, Su 12PM–5PM)* has been in vogue for decades. They also sell vintage glasses a few doors down at **Cutler & Gross Vintage** *(7 Knightsbridge Green, 020-7590-9995; hours: M–Sa 10:30AM–7PM, Su 12PM–5PM)*. The talent on Ellis Street (35) is dazzling. Ballerina shoes don't get much better than at world famous **French Sole** *(6 Ellis St., 020-7730-3771, www.frenchsole.com; hours: M–Sa 10AM–6PM, W til 6:30PM, Su 12PM–5PM)*; the delightful shop includes a line for larger sizes. **Lulu Guinness** *(3 Ellis St., 020-7823-4828, www.luluguinness.com; hours: M–Sa 10AM–6PM)* handbags, with silk flowers and embroidery, are glamorous flights of fancy. Don't miss the gems in Elizabeth Street (36). Flowers, leaves, bands, swirls, and classic chic accent the stunning hats by **Philip Treacy** *(69 Elizabeth St., 020-7730-3992, www.philiptreacy.co.uk)*. David Linley (37) *(60 Pimlico Rd., 020-7730-7300, www.davidlinley.com; hours: M–F 10AM–6PM, Sa 10AM–5PM)* finds the most finely crafted wooden furniture in diverse styles from various designers and craftsmen. Linley, Princess Margaret's son, also collects smaller decorative pieces. The fabulously creative, feminine jewelry of Lara Bohinc 107 (38) *(149F Sloane St., entrance on Sloane Terrace, 020-7730-8194, www.larabohinc107.co.uk; hours: M–Sa 10AM–6PM, W til 7PM)* has made clients of Lucy Liu, Cameron Diaz, Sarah Jessica Parker, and Björk.

WHERE TO STAY

The Berkeley (39) (£££-££££) *(Wilton Place, 020-7235-6000, www.the-berkeley.co.uk)* is among London's most luxurious and distinguished hotels. Subtle and sophisticated, it is also home to a fine restaurant and tearoom. The sumptuous **Mandarin Oriental (40) (£££-££££)** *(66 Knightsbridge, 020-7235-2000, www.mandarinoriental.com)* overlooks Hyde Park; its opulent rooms are the height of splendor.

Inside a 19th-century house, the imposing staircase of **The Diplomat (41) (££)** *(2 Chesham St., 020-7235-1544, www.thediplomathotel.co.uk)* winds its way up to lovely, large rooms. Two B&Bs on **Ebury Street (42)** provide Georgian charm, serenity, and tasteful furnishings. They are: **Morgan House (£)** *(120 Ebury St., 020-7730-2384, www.morganhouse.co.uk)*; and **Cartref House (£)** *(129 Ebury St., 020-7730-6176, www.cartrefhouse.co.uk)*. Lavishly luxurious, **The Lanesborough (43) (££££)** *(Hyde Park Corner, 020-7259-5599, www.lanesborough.com)* is a grand hotel with Regency-style decor. It even offers guests a personal butler. British charm and comfort in a town house characterize **The Capital Hotel (44) (£££-££££)** *(22 Basil St., 020-7589-5171, www.capitalhotel.co.uk)*.

CHELSEA

 Sloane Square

• SNAPSHOT •

A lovely fishing village in the 15th century, Chelsea became a draw for aristocrats, and by 1520 the likes of Sir Thomas More, Henry VIII's Lord Chancellor, lived there. Henry himself built a palace (no longer existing) in the village. Writers and intellectuals, like Thomas Carlyle and poet Swinburne, resided there, and Chelsea got a reputation as a bohemian area of artists, writers, and actors. Most famous among them were Turner, Whistler, Dante Gabriel Rossetti, his sister Christina, George Eliot, Henry James, Mark Twain, T. S. Eliot, Oscar Wilde, A. A. Milne, Hilaire Belloc, Nell Gwynne, Dame Sybil Thorndyke, and Dame Ellen Terry. It continues to be a very fashionable district, although the artists and poets are long gone. Now the stomping grounds of the young and the rich, Chelsea is famous for its blonde "Sloane Rangers" (a term describing West London's young upper- and upper-middle-class women) and boys who play polo when they're not racing their Jaguars. It overflows with chic boutiques, antiques shops, restaurants, cafés, pubs, and nightclubs, all with an approach and attitude reflecting the English balancing act between tradition and innovation.

PLACES TO SEE
Landmarks:

The 18th-century **Sloane Square (45)**, with its lovely fountain of Venus, marks the beginning of Chelsea. In the 1960s Chelsea became the rage, with the boutiques on **King's Road (46)** introducing the miniskirt and, later, punk fashions. Its side streets are charming and often reveal the unexpected: Charles Dickens was married in **St. Luke's Church** *(Sydney St.)* in 1836. Most of the 13th-century **Chelsea Old Church (47)** *(64 Cheyne Walk, parish office: 020-7795-1019, www.chelseaoldchurch.org.uk; visting hours: Tu–Th 2PM–4PM)* was destroyed in the 1941 blitz, but a replica was built. It is believed that the headless body of its most famous parishioner, Sir Thomas More, is buried there. (The head, left on a spike on London Bridge, was buried in the family tomb in Canterbury.) The church's notable Tudor statues commemorate historical figures.

Lovely **Cheyne Walk (48)** was home to many famous figures; when the Chelsea Embankment was built, traffic changed the area's character. Blue plaques, here and throughout London, mark the homes where famous people lived. **Royal Hospital Chelsea (49)** *(Royal Hospital Rd., 020-7881-5200, www.chelsea-pensioners.org.uk; hours: museum M–F 10AM–12PM, 2PM–4PM)*, designed by Sir Christopher Wren in 1692, is a home for retired soldiers. It also houses a museum and a shop. **Chelsea Physic Garden (50)** *(66 Royal Hospital Rd., entrance on Swan Walk, 020-7352-5646, www.chelseaphysicgarden.co.uk; hours: Apr–Oct Tu–F 12PM–5PM, Su 12PM–6PM)* grows medicinal herbs and vegetables and contains ancient trees and one of the first rock gardens, dating from 1772.

Arts & Entertainment:

Since its founding in 1956, the **Royal Court Theatre (51)** *(Sloane Sq., 020-7565-5000, www.royalcourttheatre.com; call for showtimes)* has been bringing exciting new play-

wrights to London theater-goers. It was here that John Osborne's *Look Back in Anger* was first staged. **Carlyle's House (52)** *(24 Cheyne Row, 020-7352-*
7087, www.nationaltrust.org.uk/carlyleshouse; hours: mid-Mar–Oct W–Su 11AM–5PM), dedicated to historian Thomas Carlyle, reveals details of life in Victorian times. The **National Army Museum (53)** *(Royal Hospital Rd., 020-7730-0717, www.nam.ac.uk; hours: daily 10AM–5:30PM)* offers an entertaining view into life in the British Army. Displays cover action from the Battle at Agincourt (1415) to the revolt of those pesky colonists, the American War of Independence.

PLACES TO EAT & DRINK
Where to Eat:

In the renovated Art Nouveau Michelin Tyre warehouse, **Bibendum Oyster Bar (54)** **(£–£££)** *(Michelin House, 81 Fulham Rd., 020-7589-1480, www.bibendum.co.uk; hours: M–Sa 12PM–11PM, Su 12PM–10:30PM)* is the brainchild of designer-entrepreneur Terence Conran. This seafood bar, in a casual patio-style setting, offers oysters, caviar, and other fabulous delicacies from the sea. Upstairs, the formal **Bibendum (££-££££)** *(020-7581-5817, www. bibendum.co.uk; hours: M–F 12PM–2:30PM, 7PM–11PM, Sa 12:30PM–3PM, 7PM–11PM, Su 12:30PM–3PM, 7PM–10:30PM)* serves New French. New French is also the creative fare at smart, sleek **Tom Aikens (55) (£££-££££)** *(43 Elystan St., 020-7584-2003, www.tomaikens.co.uk; hours: Tu–F 12PM–2:30PM, 6:30PM–10:30PM, Sa 6:30PM–10:30PM)*. Elegant, innovative Indian cuisine never disappoints at **Rasoi Vineet Bhatia (56) (££££)** *(10 Lincoln St., 020-7225-1881, www.rasoi-uk.com; hours: M–F 12PM–2:30PM, 6PM–10:30PM, Sa 6PM–10:30PM, Su 12PM–2:30PM, 6PM–9:45PM)*. The name means "Vineet Bhatia's kitchen," which is what this fabulous Delhi chef offers—in a warm, exotic dining room.

The Builders Arms (57) (££) *(13 Britten St., 020-7349-9040, www.geronimo-inns.co.uk; hours: M–W 11AM–11PM, Th–Sa 11AM–12AM, Su 12PM–10:30PM)* serves the fashionable Chelsea crowd well with great food; the big tables and comfy sofas inside, and garden tables outside, are inviting. Huge portions of Cajun cuisine, evenings of live music, and TVs showing U.S. sports are the attractions at **Big Easy (58) (£-££)** *(332-334 King's Rd., 020-7352-4071, www.bigeasy.co.uk; hours: M–Th 12PM–11PM, F–Sa 12PM–12AM, Su 12PM–10:30PM)*.

BARS & NIGHTLIFE:

The **Admiral Codrington (59)** *(17 Mossop St., 020-7581-0005, www.theadmiralcodrington.co.uk; hours: M–Tu 11:30AM–11PM, W–Th 11:30AM–12AM, F–Sa*

11:30AM–1AM, Su 12PM–10:30PM) established itself years ago as a local favorite. Authentic with tiled interior, the **Chelsea Potter (60)** *(119 King's Rd., 020-7352-9479; hours: Su–F 11AM–11PM, Sa 11AM–12AM)* swells with fans who love its laid-back, unpretentious style. Young, rich Chelsea fashionistas hop from club to bar, stopping at **Latitude (61)** *(163-165 Draycott Ave., 020-7589-8464; call for hours)*, one of the "reserved-for-only-the-cool" spots. When the clubs and bars close shop, there's always **Vingt-Quatre (62)** *(325 Fulham Rd., 020-7376-7224, www.vq24hours. com; hours: open 24/7)*, a trendy all-night bar-café.

WHERE TO SHOP

Sloane Square (45) *(see page 99)* marks the beginning of a network of streets full of designer boutiques, home furnishings, accessories, and antiques. **David Mellor** *(4 Sloane Sq., 020-7730-4259, www.davidmellordesign. com; hours: M–Sa 9:30AM–6PM, Su 11AM–5PM)* designs include cutlery, tableware, and kitchen implements. If the boutique prices of the area make your head spin, try the department store **Peter Jones** *(Sloane Sq., 020-7730-3434, www.johnlewis.com; hours: M–Sa 9:30AM–7PM, W till 8PM, Su 11AM–5PM)*. **King's Road (46)** *(see page 99)*, another shopper's mecca, has high-end fashion, interior furnishings, gifts, and antiques. Another area of antiques shops is **Royal Hospital Road**.

Manolo Blahnik (63) *(49-51 Old Church St., 020-7352-8622, www.manoloblahnik.com)* shoes are wearable art; the stunning store displays are too tempting. Along Fulham Road (64), **Margaret Howell** *(111 Fulham Rd., 020-7591-2255, www.margarethowell.co.uk; hours: M–Sa 10AM–6PM, W till 7PM, Su 12PM–5PM)* designs relaxed styles with a classic bent, for men and women, as well as objects for the home. **Butler & Wilson** *(189 Fulham Rd., 020-7352-3045, www.butlerandwilson.co.uk; hours: M–Sa 10AM–6PM, W till 7PM, Su 12PM–6PM)* is a treasure trove of costume jewelry. Rugs designed by Christopher Farr (65) *(6 Burnsall St., 020-7349-0888, www.christopherfarr.com)* are truly works of art; the shop also sells limited edition contemporary rugs by other top designers.

WHERE TO STAY

Cadogan Gardens (66) is a quiet, discreet street. Four Victorian houses make up **Eleven Cadogan Gardens (££-£££)** *(11 Cadogan Gdns., 020-7730-7000, www.no11cadogangardens.com)*. Its understated elegance and impeccable service are the hallmarks of an authentically English aristocratic experience. The **Draycott Hotel (££-£££)** *(26 Cadogan Gdns., 020-7730-6466, www.draycotthotel.com)* has the comfort and charm of a country house. **San Domenico House (67) (£££)** *(29-31 Draycott Pl., 020-7581-5757, www.sandomenicohouse.com)* offers roomy accommodations with antique furniture in a Victorian house; the rooftop terrace is an added delight.

chapter 4

KENSINGTON & HOLLAND PARK

NOTTING HILL & BAYSWATER

Rd.

KENSINGTON & HOLLAND PARK NOTTING HILL & BAYSWATER

Places to See:

1. Kensington Square
2. Kensington Roof Gardens
3. Holland Park
4. Holland House
5. Linley Sambourne House
6. Leighton House Museum
7. Holland Park Theatre
16. Portobello Road
17. Electric Cinema
18. Notting Hill Tour
19. Queensway

Places to Eat & Drink:

8. Zaika
9. Maggie Jones
10. Belvedere
11. Windsor Castle
12. The Scarsdale Tavern
21. Beach Blanket Babylon
22. Electric Diner
23. The Cow
24. Lucky 7
25. Golborne Road
26. Trailer Happiness
27. Lonsdale
28. Under the Westway
42. Geales
45. Babylon

Where to Shop:

13. Kensington Church Street
20. Ben Day
29. Vessel
30. Paul Smith
31. Rough Trade
32. Portobello Green
33. Dinny Hall
34. Ledbury Road
35. Needham Road
36. Cath Kidston
37. Clarendon Cross
38. Portland Road
39. Porchester Spa

Where to Stay:

14. Milestone Hotel
15. EasyHotel
40. Abbey Court
41. Portobello Gold
43. The Portobello
44. The Main House

⊖ *High Street Kensington,*
Holland Park, Notting Hill Gate

● SNAPSHOT ●

When Edward the Confessor ventured beyond the City of London into what was then countryside to build Westminster Abbey and the Palace of Westminster in the 11th century, a westward movement began, incorporating villages into the capital. Urban sprawl continued well beyond Westminster, St. James's, Mayfair, and Belgravia. West London's wealthy, quiet Kensington is home to several foreign embassies, and its chic shops nearly compare to those of Knightsbridge. The beautiful Victorian houses of upscale Holland Park surround this green oasis with the gentility expected by the upper-class English.

PLACES TO SEE
Landmarks:

Lovely old **Kensington Square (1)** attracted intellectuals and luminaries in ages past. Thackeray lived at No. 16; John Stuart Mill at No. 18; and Pre-Raphaelite painter

Edward Burne-Jones at No. 41. A little-known Eden, the **Kensington Roof Gardens (2)** *(99 Kensington High St., entrance in Derry St., 020-7937-7994, www.roofgardens.com; call for*

hours) include woodlands, palm trees, a formal garden, and a pond with ducks and flamingos. If you prefer *terra firma*, **Holland Park (3)** *(Abbotsbury Rd., 020-7361-3003, www.rbkc.gov.uk; hours: daily 7:30AM–30 min. before dusk)* is lovely and intimate. The bridge and waterfall in the **Japanese Garden** are especially pleasant, while wooded areas provide shelter for many animals, including rabbits and peacocks. The park was built on the grounds of **Holland House (4)** *(Holland Park, 020-7361-3003; call for hours)*, the front terrace of which is the stage for summer concerts and theater. The garden ballroom houses a restaurant, and the east wing is a youth hostel.

Arts & Entertainment:

Linley Sambourne House (5) *(18 Stafford Terr., 020-7602-3316, www.rbkc.gov.uk/linleysambournehouse, guided tours only, book ahead; hours: W 11:15AM, 2:15PM, Sa–Su 11:15AM, costumed tours Sa–Su 1PM, 2:15PM, & 3:30PM, private guided tours by appt., groups of 12-30)*, the *Punch* magazine cartoonist's Victorian home, William Morris wallpaper and all, features its owner's satirical drawings. The home of another Victorian artist, **Leighton House Museum (6)** *(12 Holland Park Rd., 020-7602-3316, www.rbkc.gov.uk/leightonhousemuseum; hours: W–M 10AM–5:30PM, free guided tour W & Su 3PM)* pays homage to 19th-century decorative arts and interior design. The museum's most spectacular room is the Arab Hall, an elaborate Moorish-style room with a fountain, mosaic floor, cupola, and stained glass. The collection of 16th- and 17th-century Damascus tiles is the most significant in Britain. **Holland Park Theatre (7)** *(Holland Park, info: 020-7361-3570, box office & picnic reserva-*

tions 0300-999-1000, www.operahollandpark.com; hours: daily 6PM–10/10:30PM, open 5:30PM for reserved dining) stages opera in the park during the summer.

PLACES TO EAT & DRINK
Where to Eat:

Zaika (8) (££-£££) *(1 Kensington High St., 020-7795-6533, www.zaika-restaurant.co.uk; hours: M 5:30PM–10:45PM, Tu-Sa 12PM–2:45PM, 5:30PM–10:45PM, Su 12PM–2:45PM, 5:30PM–9:45PM)* offers tasting menus (five or nine courses) to sample its Indian haute cuisine. **Zaika (8)** and **Rasoi Vineet Bhatia** *(see page 101)* were both started by award-winning Chef Vineet Bhatia. Rustic and quaint, **Maggie Jones (9) (£-££)** *(6 Old Court Pl., Kensington Church St., 020-7937-6462, www.maggie-jones.co.uk; hours: M–Sa 12:30PM–2:30PM, 6:30PM–11PM, Su 12:30PM–2:30PM, 6:30PM–10:30PM)* has been serving the same good food for some 40 years. Try the prawn cocktail, fish pie, or poached salmon. Restaurateur Marco Pierre White's **Belvedere (10) (£££££)** *(Holland Park, off Abbotsbury Rd., 020-7602-1238, belvedererestaurant.co.uk; hours: M–Sa 12PM–2:30PM, 6PM–11PM, Su 12PM–3:30PM)* is a huge Modern British/New French hit. Situated in Holland Park's Holland House, it feels like an elegant country home engulfed by gardens. From fish and chips to seafood platters, **Geales (42) (£-£££)** *(2 Farmer St., 020-7727-7528, www.geales.com; hours: M 6PM–10:30PM, Tu-Sa 12PM–3PM, 6PM–10:30PM, Su 12PM–9:30PM)* is a snazzy eatery opened by food mavens Mark Fuller and Andy Taylor. Chic black leather banquettes and wood paneling are tempered by checked tablecloths for an elegant but laid-back ambience. The best of British fish and chips or a salad and lobster or rib-eye steak make a satisfying meal. Chic and modern, **Babylon (45)** **(££–£££)** *(99 Kensington High St., entrance in Derry St., 020-7368-3993, www.roofgardens.virgin.com; hours: M–Sa 12PM–2:30PM, 7PM–10:30PM, Su 12PM–2:30PM)* serves delicious haute cuisine meals in a fabulous panoramic setting, the Kensington Rooftop Gardens. Tuesday nights there's live jazz.

Bars & Nightlife:

Windsor Castle (11) *(114 Campden Hill Rd., 020-7243-8797, www.thewindsorcastlekensington.co.uk; hours: M–Sa 12PM–11PM, Su 12PM–10:30PM)* has an old pub atmosphere, with dark wood paneling and a lovely garden. In posh Kensington, **The Scarsdale Tavern (12)** *(23a Edwardes Sq., 020-7937-1811, www.scarsdaletavern. co.uk; hours: M–Sa 12PM–11PM, Su 12PM–10:30PM)* is a friendly place with a serene, home-style atmosphere; it also serves food.

WHERE TO SHOP

More than 80 superb antiques shops line beautiful Kensington Church Street (13). The goods are fine quality and the dealers friendly. For more shopping head to Notting Hill & Bayswater *(see page 113)*.

WHERE TO STAY

The Milestone Hotel (14) **(££££)** *(1 Kensington Ct., 020-7917-1000, www.milestonehotel.com)* is a boutique hotel with oak-paneled lounge and elegantly decorated bedrooms. Despite small rooms, budget rates are the draw at **EasyHotel (15)** **(£)** *(14 Lexham Gdns., www.easyhotel.com)*.

NOTTING HILL & BAYSWATER

⊖ *Notting Hill Gate, Holland Park, Ladbroke Grove,
Westbourne Park, Bayswater, Queensway, Lancaster Gate*

• SNAPSHOT •

A few streets north of Holland Park, but light years away,
is Notting Hill. Funky and arty, the once poverty-stricken
working-class neighborhood has been gentrified, and
bohemian trust fund kids mesh with an edgy artistic and
alternative designer scene. The West Indian immigrants
who once lived in Notting Hill inaugurated the late-
August carnival that still celebrates Afro-Caribbean culture. The famous Portobello Road, with its weekend
antiques and flea market, is the main artery of a warren
of streets whose galleries, boutiques, and eateries are the
turf of street-smart urban cognoscenti. Bayswater, to the
east, is full of Victorian houses long ago converted into
apartments or hotels. These less expensive hotels retain a
modicum of charm and are still close enough to the
main sights.

PLACES TO SEE
Landmarks:
Portobello Road (16) (*www.portobello
road.co.uk*) is a great antiques street market on Saturdays, with antiques shops
open all week. It's more interesting north
of Chepstow Villas; side streets are full of

fascinating stores, sights, and a street-chic vibe. The **Electric Cinema (17)** *(see below)*, a legendary movie theater, is Britain's oldest working one. Take the **Notting Hill Tour (18)** *(59 Notting Hill Gate, 0844-247-1007, britmovie tours.com/bookings/notting-hill-movie-tour; hours: Apr–Sep once/month 11AM)* to see where Hugh Grant and Julia Roberts met in the film *Notting Hill*, along with other local landmarks and homes of celebrities, the likes of Elle MacPherson and Richard Branson. Bayswater's main street, **Queensway (19)**, named in honor of Queen Victoria, is packed with eateries, newsagents selling foreign newspapers, and, at the north end, **Whiteley's**, thought to be the world's first department store, now a mall.

Arts & Entertainment:

For years the **Electric Cinema (17)** *(191 Portobello Rd., 020-7908-9696, www.electriccinema.co.uk; call for showtimes)* has been a favorite movie theater among film buffs. Now refurbished, it has leather armchairs, footstools, and even tables for your movie snacks. Its **Electric Scream** program projects films for kids.

PLACES TO EAT & DRINK
Where to Eat:

Notting Hill overflows with restaurants and cafés. Also browse **Westbourne Grove**, which boasts a number of good restaurants.

Beach Blanket Babylon (21) (££-£££) *(45 Ledbury Rd., 020-7229-2907, www.beachblanket.co.uk; hours: daily 12PM–12AM)* serves up atmosphere in an old Georgian house with various rooms connected via walkways, tunnels, and bridges, complete with large fireplaces.

The **Electric Diner (22) (£–££)** *(191 Portobello Rd., 020-7908-9696, www.electricdiner.com; hours: M–Th 8AM–12AM, F–Su 8AM–1AM)* is usually packed and has a wide range of choices, from burgers to seafood. **Westbourne Park Road** is an important restaurant street. One of London's great gastropubs, **The Cow (23) (£–££)** *(89 Westbourne Park Rd., 020-7221-0021, www.thecow london.co.uk; hours: M–F 7PM–11PM, Sa 12PM–3PM, 7PM–11PM, Su 12PM–3PM, 7PM–10:30PM)* specializes in seafood and is renowned for its oysters and Guinness. Under owner Tom Conran (son of designer-restaurateur Terence Conran), it's become so famous that Hugh Grant, Uma Thurman, Elvis Costello, and Kylie Minogue, among others, have been spotted there. **Lucky 7 (24) (£)** *(127 Westbourne Park Rd., 020-7727-6771, www.lucky7london.co.uk; call for hours)*, the Brit design version of an American diner, is a burger joint with eggs and pancakes for breakfast. Also check out **Golborne Road (25)** for good eating spots. It's a bit further away, but is worth the trek.

Bars & Nightlife:

A cross between trailer home and tropical kitsch, **Trailer Happiness (26)** *(177 Portobello Rd., 020-7313-4644, www.trailerh.com; hours: Tu–Sa 5PM–12AM)* is a hip, friendly place. An arty clientele fills the stylish **Lonsdale (27)** *(48 Lonsdale Rd., 020-7727-4080, www.thelonsdale. co.uk; hours: Tu–Th 6PM–12AM, F–Sa 6PM–1AM)*—book ahead! **Under the Westway (28)** *(Westbourne Studios, 242 Acklam Rd., 020-7575-3123; hours: M–Th 8:30AM–8PM, F 8:30AM–2:30AM, Sa 9PM–2:30AM)* is a hip concept in the Westbourne Studios, an agglomeration of studios and small businesses: it's a bar, performance/exhibition space, and restaurant combined.

WHERE TO SHOP

Jewelry designer **Ben Day (20)** *(3 Lonsdale Rd., 020-3417-3873, www.benday.co.uk; hours: Tu–Sa 11AM–6PM, Su 11AM–5PM)* creates exquisite pieces with precious metals, gems, and pearls. The outstanding glass and ceramics at **Vessel (29)** *(114 Kensington Park Rd., 020-7727-8001, www.vesselgallery.com; hours: M–Sa 10AM–6PM)* are the work of great contemporary designers. The **Paul Smith (30)** *(Westbourne House, 122 Kensington Park Rd., 020-7727-3553, www.paulsmith.co.uk; hours: M–F 10AM–6PM, Sa 10AM–6:30PM, Su 12PM–5PM)* line is presented in a beautiful Victorian house. Buy the latest musical recordings at **Rough Trade (31)** *(130 Talbot Rd., 020-7229-8541, www.rough trade.com; hours: M–Sa 10AM–6:30PM, Su 11AM–5PM)*. **Portobello Green (32)** *(281 Portobello Rd., www.portobello designers.com)*, an arcade under the Westway flyover, is home to a variety of young designers and attractive shops, including **Preen**, **Sarah Bunting**, **In Bloom London**, and **Zarvis**. Besides eateries, **Westbourne Grove** is full of shops. The handmade jewelry of **Dinny Hall (33)** *(200 Westbourne Grove, 020-7792-3913, www.dinnyhall.com; hours: M, Tu, W, F 10AM–6:30PM, Th 10AM–7PM, Sa 10AM–6PM, Su 12PM–5PM)* is displayed at the Tate Modern.

Innovative shops dot Ledbury Road (34): **Doyle Devere** *(30 Ledbury Rd., 020-7243-6628, www.doyledevere. co.uk; hours: W–Sa 12PM–6PM, Su 12PM–4PM)* showcases exciting contemporary art and photography by both established and emerging artists.

Tiny Needham Road (35) contains plenty of treasures: extraordinary British applied arts at **Flow** *(1-5 Needham Rd., 020-7243-0782, www.flowgallery.co.uk; hours: M–Sa 11AM–6PM, Su by appt)*; and ready-made and bespoke perfumes at **Miller Harris** *(14 Needham Rd., 020-7221-1545, www.millerharris.com; hours: M–Sa 10AM–6PM)*. The linens, home accessories, and fabrics of Cath Kidston (36) *(158 Portobello Rd., 020-7727-0043, www.cathkidston.co.uk; hours: M–F 10AM–6PM, Sa 9AM–7PM, Su 11AM–6PM)* are quintessentially English. On Clarendon Cross (37) and Portland Road (38) *(www.clarendoncross.net)* shops are both nostalgic and stylish. And after a long day of shopping, head to Porchester Spa (39) *(The Porchester Centre, Queensway, 020-7792-2919, www.better.org.uk/leisure/porchester-centre; hours: M–F 6:30AM–10PM, Sa–Su 8AM–8PM; hours vary by gender)*. It's one of London's few remaining Turkish baths: get steamed, scrubbed, and massaged 'til you glow. Take an exercise class or have a dip in the pool.

WHERE TO STAY

Abbey Court (40) (£-££) *(20 Pembridge Gdns., 020-7221-7518, www.abbeycourthotel.co.uk)*, a friendly, beautiful town house, has charming rooms. **Portobello Gold (41)** (£-££) *(95-97 Portobello Rd., 020-7460-4910, www.portobellogold.com)* is a pub with well-kept, modernized rooms upstairs. **The Portobello (43)** (££-£££) *(22 Stanley Gdns., 020-7727-2777, www.portobello-hotel.co.uk)* combines a friendly atmosphere with quirky elegance.

At **The Main House (44)** (£-££) *(6 Colville Rd., 020-7221-9691, www.themainhouse.co.uk; minimum 3 nights)*, an unassuming, unfussy Victorian house, large rooms are sparingly decorated.

chapter 5

MARYLEBONE

BLOOMSBURY & FITZROVIA

MARYLEBONE
BLOOMSBURY & FITZROVIA

Places to See:

1. Park Crescent
2. Royal Institute of British Architects (RIBA)
3. Broadcasting House
4. All Souls
5. St. Marylebone Parish Church
6. Regent's Park
7. London Zoo
8. London Central Mosque
9. Cumberland Terrace
10. Regent's Canal
11. Madame Tussauds
12. Sherlock Holmes Museum
13. Wallace Collection
14. Wigmore Hall
36. Bloomsbury Square
37. Bedford Square
38. Russell Square
39. Fitzroy Square
40. BRITISH MUSEUM ★
41. Cartoon Museum
42. Charles Dickens Museum
43. Foundling Museum
44. St. Pancras Parish Church
46. Pollock's Toy Museum

Places to Eat & Drink:

15. Fairuz
16. Langan's Bistro
17. La Fromagerie
18. Orrery
19. Providores/Tapa Room
20. Özer
21. Dover Castle
22. Golden Eagle
45. North Sea Fish Restaurant
47. Charlotte Street:
    Roka
    Fino
48. Bam-Bou
49. Pho
50. Hakkasan
51. Fitzroy Tavern
52. The Social
53. Duke (of York)
54. The Lamb

Where to Shop:

23. Gallery 1930
24. Chiltern Street
25. Vaishaly Patel
26. Mascaró
27. Daunt Books

★ *Top Pick*

It's elementary, my dear Watson.

—Attributed to Sir Arthur Conan Doyle's
Sherlock Holmes

MARYLEBONE

• SNAPSHOT •

Beautiful Georgian homes, manicured lawns, and neo-classical buildings set the tone for the high-class Marylebone area. The quiet neighborhood, once a medieval village, has retained its small-town flavor. Bow windows, wrought-iron balconies, and stucco terraces grace homes along picturesque squares. Harley Street, famous for its upscale private (non-National Health System) doctors, once counted Wellington, Turner, Gladstone, and Florence Nightingale among its residents. This is the neighborhood of Sherlock Holmes, Madame Tussauds, and the Wallace Collection. To the north is Regent's Park, a gorgeous land-scaped garden of flowers, trees, waterways, and bucolic paths. Birds, ducks, swans, fish, and turtles provide constant entertainment.

PLACES TO SEE
Landmarks:

Outside Regent's Park Tube stop is one of the most breath-taking spots of London: **Park Crescent (1)** *(off Marylebone Rd.)*—a semicircle of colonnades designed by John Nash. His majestic façades remain intact though the interiors of the buildings were redone in the 1960s. This was the culmination of the ceremonial route Nash built from St. James's to Regent's Park, via Regent Street and the equally beautiful **Portland Place**. The statues and reliefs on the Art Deco building of the **Royal Institute of British Architects (RIBA) (2)** *(66 Portland Pl., 020-7580-5533, www. architecture.com; hours: M–F 9:30AM–5:30PM, Sa 10AM– 5PM)* are symbolic of the métier and the world's most influential architectural association. The BBC's **Broadcasting House (3)** *(Portland Pl., not open to public; Backstage tours, 0370-901-1227, www.bbc.co.uk/tours, daily tours; also for tours of BBC TV Centre, Wood Lane, in West London, White City Tube stop, daily tours)* is another Art Deco masterpiece with sculptures by Eric Gill. **All Souls (4)** *(Langham Place, 020-7580-3522, www.allsouls.org; reception hours: Su 9AM–2PM, 5:30PM–8:30PM, weekdays 9:30AM–5:30PM)*, the only church built by John Nash, is surprising: it combines a classical rotunda and columns with a Gothic spire.

Posh **Harley Street** runs parallel to Portland Place. Once home to notables such as Prime Minister Gladstone (No. 73), Wellington (No. 11), and Turner (No. 64), it is renowned as the street of private physicians. Elizabeth Barrett lived in Wimpole Street before eloping to marry Robert Browning in the grand **St. Marylebone Parish Church (5)** *(Marylebone Rd., 020-7935-7315, www.stmarylebone.org; call for hours)*. Charles Dickens lived in a house that once stood on the site of the church. Visitors can see a panel depicting characters from several of his works. When Conan Doyle invented **221B Baker Street** as legendary detective Sherlock Holmes's residence, the address didn't exist. But the street was renumbered in 1930, and *voilà!* Sherlock has a home! It's now a museum *(see page 122)*.

Dazzling Regency villas bordering **Regent's Park (6)** *(0300-061-2300, www.royalparks.org.uk; hours: daily 5AM–dusk)* were part of Nash's brilliant design for one of London's most incredible parks. Formal, botanical, and zoological gardens coexist with a boating lake, playing fields, and an open-air theater. The park's rose gardens include over 400 varieties of roses. It is home to the fascinating **London Zoo (7)** *(Regent's Park, Outer Circle, 0844-225-1826, 020-7722-3333, www.zsl.org/london-zoo; hours: daily early Mar–mid-July, Sept–Oct 10AM–5:30PM, mid-July–Aug 10AM–6PM, Nov–mid-Feb 10AM–4PM, mid-Feb–early Mar 10AM–5PM)*, also a conservation center. On the park's west side is **London Central Mosque (8)** *(146 Park Rd., 020-7725-2212, www.iccuk.org; call for hours)*; to the east is Nash's magnificent **Cumberland Terrace (9)** *(Regent's Park, Outer Circle)*, with its raised Ionic columns and a fabulously ornate pediment. Nash created **Regent's Canal (10)** *(Waterbus: info: 020-7482-2660, bookings: 020-7482-2550, www.londonwaterbus.co.uk)*, which opened in 1820, both to enhance the park and to connect East and West London. The stretch between Little Venice and Camden Lock is especially lovely.

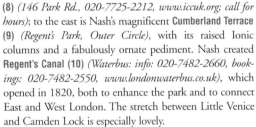

Arts & Entertainment:

Famous people are gathered at **Madame Tussauds (11)** *(Marylebone Rd. at Baker St., 0871-894-3000, www.madametussauds.com; hours: M–F 9:30AM–5:30PM, Sa–Su 9AM–6PM)* wax museum; from the Henrys to Queen Elizabeth, from Shakespeare to Beyoncé, leaders of politics, arts, sports, and history seem to come alive. Interactive rooms make you feel part of the action. The **Planetarium** next door is part of the show too. The **Sherlock Holmes Museum**

(12) *(221b Baker St., 020-7224-3688, www.sherlock-holmes.co.uk; hours: daily 9:30AM–6PM)* is designed and furnished the way the famous detective's flat is described in Conan Doyle's classic novels. Impressive artworks in a late-18th-century town house rank the **Wallace Collection (13)** *(Hertford House, Manchester Sq., 020-7563-9500, www.wallacecollection.org; hours: daily 10AM–5PM)* among the capital's finest museums. Old Masters, 18th-century French paintings, furniture, porcelain, and an armory are its highlights. The intimate concert venue **Wigmore Hall (14)** *(36 Wigmore St., 020-7935-2141, www.wigmore-hall.org.uk; box office hours: daily 10AM–5PM, 10AM–8:30PM on concert evenings)* presents chamber music and recitals.

PLACES TO EAT & DRINK
Where to Eat:

The Lebanese dishes at **Fairuz (15) (£–££)** *(3 Blandford St., 020-7486-8108, www.fairuz.uk.com; hours: M–Sa 12PM–11PM, Su 12PM–10:30PM)* are fantastic: the *mezze*—small hors d'oeuvres of tabouleh, falafel, and such—can make a meal; or try the grilled foods, smoked cod roe, or chicken wings. Cozy **Langan's Bistro (16) (££)** *(26 Devonshire St., 020-7935-4531, www.langansrestaurants.co.uk; hours: M–F 12PM–2:30PM, 6:30PM–11PM, Sa 6:30PM–11PM)* has a traditional French and British menu and unusual artwork on the walls. For great salads, cheeses, and desserts, head for charming **La Fromagerie (17) (£)** *(2-6 Moxon St., 020-7935-0341, www.lafromagerie.co.uk; hours: M–F 8AM–7:30PM, Sa 9AM–7PM, Su 10AM–6PM)*. The slick Conran eatery **Orrery (18) (££-£££)** *(55 Marylebone High St., 020-7616-8000, www.orreryrestaurant.co.uk; hours: M–Th 12PM–2:30PM, 6:30PM–10PM, F–Sa 12PM–2:30PM, 6:30PM–10:30PM, Su 12PM–3PM, 6:30PM–10PM)* serves New French with panache; the rest of the drama is provided by the chic patrons. Truly a gourmet adventure, the **Providores/Tapa Room (19) (££-£££)** *(109 Marylebone High St., 020-7935-6175, www.theprovidores.co.uk; Providores hours: M–F 12PM–2:45PM, 6PM–10:30PM, Sa 11AM–2:45PM, 6PM–10:30PM, Su 11AM–2:45PM, 6PM–10PM; Tapa Room hours: M–F 9AM–11:30AM, 12PM–10:30PM, Sa 10AM–3PM, 4PM–10:30PM, Su 10AM–3PM, 4PM–10PM)* mixes unusual, exotic foods for a memorable culinary experience in a hip, exciting venue. One of London's best Turkish restaurants, **Özer (20) (£-££)** *(5 Langham Pl., 020-7323-0505, www.sofra.co.uk; call for hours)* excels in Mediterranean cuisine, from the mixed *borek* platter to the grilled fish and vegetables; copper and scarlet walls add exoticism.

Bars & Nightlife:

Neighborhood locals gather at the rustic Georgian pub **Dover Castle (21)** *(43 Weymouth Mews, 020-7580-4412; hours: M–Sa 12PM–11PM)*; dating from 1777, it offers an authentic London experience. Community reigns at the **Golden Eagle (22)** *(59 Marylebone Ln., 020-7935-3228; hours: M–Sa 11AM–11PM, Su 12PM–7PM)*, where patrons cluster around the piano and sing together.

WHERE TO SHOP

The Art Deco ceramics, lamps, and furniture at Gallery 1930 (23) *(18 Church St., 020-7723-1555; hours: Tu–Sa 10AM–5PM)* comprise a rich variety of 1930s pieces. Check out other antiques dealers in Church Street and **Alfie's**, the cluster of antiques stalls. The shops in Chiltern Street (24) specialize in custom-made wedding and formal fashions and musical instruments. Beauty treatments is what Vaishaly Patel (25) *(51 Paddington St., 020-7224-6088, www.vaishaly.com)* calls her salon services; others say it's magic. Besides facials, she offers microdermabrasion, lymphatic stimulation, and Chinese medical procedures. RIBA (2) *(see page 120)* has an incredible architecture bookshop *(020-7307-3753; hours: M–F 9:30AM–5:30PM, Sa 10AM–5PM)*.

Though **Marylebone High Street** has become a fashionable strip, it hasn't lost its village atmosphere. The fabulous, colorful, sexy shoes and handbags of Spanish designer Mascaró (26) *(13a Marylebone High St., 020-7935-1795, www.jaimemascaro.com; call for hours)* have been sported by Kate Moss, Claudia Schiffer, Katherine Heigl, and Kylie Minogue, among others. Among the picturesque shops and cafés, Daunt Books (27) *(83 Marylebone High St., 020-7224-2295, www.dauntbooks.co.uk; hours: M–Sa 9AM–7:30PM, Su 11AM–6PM)* is stunning in its Edwardian beauty—a fabulous atrium runs the length of the shop, and books on travel, cooking, and literature nestle in oak galleries. Kabiri (28) *(37 Marylebone High St., 020-7317-2150, www.kabiri.co.uk; hours: M–Sa 10AM–7PM, Su 12PM–6PM)* will satisfy jewelry lovers with its collection of baubles from established and emerging designers encompassing all price points. Visit **Le Petit Chou (29)** *(15 St. Christopher's Pl., 020-7486-3637, petitchou.co.uk; hours: M–Sa 10:30AM–6:30PM, Su 12PM–5PM)* for European-styled children's clothes and colorful wooden toys. **Selfridges (30)** *(400 Oxford St., 0800-123-400, www.selfridges.co.uk; hours: M–Tu 9:30AM–8PM, W–Sa 9:30AM–9PM, Su 11:30AM–6PM)*, the famous department store, has British design at reasonable prices and a great food hall. **Browns Labels for Less (31)** *(60 Marylebone Lane, 020-7514-0052, www.brownsfashion.com; hours: M–Sa 10:30AM–7PM)* sells discounted designer clothing for women and men. **Oxford Street** is one of London's shopping meccas.

WHERE TO STAY

In two beautiful Georgian town houses, the B&B **22 York Street (32)** **(£-££)** *(22-24 York St., 020-7224-2990, www.22yorkstreet.co.uk)* offers flair with its antiques and cozy furnishings. For typical English charm, **Durrants Hotel (33)** **(££-£££)** *(26-32 George St., 020-7935-8131, www.durrantshotel.co.uk)* has been serving up nostalgia since 1790. Large rooms and modern amenities, including pool and sauna, make **The Marylebone Hotel (34)** **(££-£££)** *(47 Welbeck St., 020-7486-6600, www.doyle collection.com)* an updated hotel in classic, tasteful surroundings. **The Langham Hotel (35)** **(£££-££££)** *(1c Portland Pl., 020-7636-1000, www.langhamhotels.com)* has been providing high luxury and stylish accommodations since 1865; the spa is fit for a sybarite and the tea-time pianist plays soothingly. No wonder Oscar Wilde, Antonin Dvořák, and Mark Twain stayed there.

BLOOMSBURY & FITZROVIA

⊖ *Tottenham Court Road, Russell Square,*
Goodge Street, Warren Street, Euston Square, Euston,
King's Cross–St. Pancras

• SNAPSHOT •

Since the early-20th century, Bloomsbury has been intrinsically tied to the Bloomsbury Group of writers and artists, including Virginia Woolf, E. M. Forster, Clive and Vanessa Bell, Duncan Grant, Roger Fry, and Lytton Strachey, among others. Besides literature and  art, the neighborhood's intellectual reputation is upheld by the University of London campus and a clutch of museums, most notably the British Museum. Fashionably shabby, Bloomsbury continues to be a draw for the intelligentsia. Fitzrovia, west of Bloomsbury, may have gotten its name from Fitzroy Square. Some believe the name came from the Fitzroy Tavern, where Dylan Thomas, George Orwell, Quentin Crisp, Aleister Crowley, and their cohorts went drinking. The bohemian allure remains but the dominant artistic domain has shifted from literature to music, while Charlotte Street, a Fitzrovia destination, is known for its ethnic restaurants.

PLACES TO SEE
Landmarks:

The trend for beautiful squares was set in the area in 1661 by **Bloomsbury Square (36)**. Many blue plaques throughout Bloomsbury and Fitzrovia mark places where significant writers, artists, and intellectuals lived. These include William Butler Yeats, Mary Wollstonecraft, Edgar Allan Poe, Anthony Trollope, Charles Dickens, Bloomsbury Group members mentioned above, as well as John Maynard Keynes, D. H. Lawrence, Rupert Brooke, and Bertrand Russell, among other notables. **Bedford Square (37)**, a grand Georgian square of 18th-century houses, is an elegant array of brick buildings with rounded doorways topped by fanlights and pediment centerpieces and embellished by wrought-iron balconies and window grates. In **Russell Square (38)** the **Hotel Russell (65)** *(see page 133)*, built by Charles Doll in 1900, is a large terra-cotta construction with colonnaded balconies, cherubs, and fairy-tale-like rooftop designs.

Beautiful, stately **Fitzroy Square (39)** is replete with blue plaques marking the homes of famous writers, artists, and statesmen. At different times, George Bernard Shaw lived at 29 Fitzroy Square, as did Virginia Woolf. Roger Fry set up the Omega workshop at No. 33, where young artists made paintings, ceramics, furniture, and carpets.

Arts & Entertainment:

TOP PICK!

Founded in 1753, the ★**BRITISH MUSEUM (40)** *(Great Russell St., 020-7323-8299, www.britishmuseum.org; hours: daily 10AM–5:30PM, F til 8:30PM)* is the world's oldest public museum. Its treasures date from prehistory to the present; highlights include the Rosetta Stone, Egyptian mummies, sculptures from the Parthenon, and the 2,000-year-old sacrificial human "Lindow Man." For the millennium, the museum's Queen Elizabeth II Great Court was unveiled. Sir Norman Foster's lightweight glass and steel roof spans the entire courtyard, making it the largest covered public

square in Europe. At the courtyard's center is the former "study room" of Karl Marx, George Bernard Shaw, Mahatma Gandhi, and others—the British Library, beautifully restored to its 19th-century magnificence.

At the **Cartoon Museum (41)** *(35 Little Russell St., 020-7580-8155, www.cartoonmuseum.org; hours: M–Sa 10:30AM–5:30PM, Su 12PM–5:30PM)* British cartoons, caricatures, and comic art from the 18th century to the present are on display; cartooning workshops are held for children and adults. The **Charles Dickens Museum (42)** *(48 Doughty St., 020-7405-2127, www.dickensmuseum.com; hours: daily 10AM–5PM)*, where the novelist wrote *Oliver Twist* and *Nicholas Nickleby*, displays Dickens memorabilia. The **Foundling Museum (43)** *(40 Brunswick Sq.,*

020-7841-3600, *www.foundlingmuseum.org.uk; hours: Tu–Sa 10AM–5PM, Su 11AM–5PM)* focuses on the Foundling Hospital, established in 1739 to care for the shocking numbers of abandoned children. The foundation soon began receiving art paintings as donations, turning it into London's first public gallery.

The dignified Greek revival **St. Pancras Parish Church (44)** *(Euston Rd., 020-7388-1461, www.stpancras church.org; call for hours)* holds lunchtime recitals *(Th 1:15pm)*. Toys from around the world animate **Pollock's Toy Museum (46)** *(1 Scala St., 020-7636-3452, www.pollockstoymuseum.com; hours: M–Sa 10AM–5PM)*, including Victorian dollhouses and pieces from Benjamin Pollock's famous toy theaters. If you're lucky, you might catch a free puppet show, performed at various times throughout the year.

PLACES TO EAT & DRINK
Where to Eat:
The **Charlotte Street (47)** domain is ethnic gastronomy. **Roka (£££–££££)** *(37 Charlotte St., 020-7580-6464, www. rokarestaurant.com; hours: M–F 12PM–3:30PM, 5:30PM– 11:30PM, Sa 12:30PM–4PM, 5:30PM–11:30PM, Su 12:30PM–4PM, 5:30PM–10:30PM)*, serves robata grilled dishes, sushi, and tempura. **Fino (££–£££)** *(33 Charlotte St., entrance on Rathbone St., 020-7813-8010, www.fino restaurant.com; hours: M–F 12PM–2:30PM, 6PM–10:30PM, Sa 6PM–10:30PM)* specializes in divine tapas dishes and other Spanish fare. In a romantic colonial-style town house

full of intimate nooks and multiple rooms, **Bam-Bou (48)** **(£-££)** *(1 Percy St., 020-7323-9130, www.bam-bou.co.uk; hours: M–Sa 12PM–11PM)* comes up with delicious Vietnamese dishes.

Inspired Vietnamese dishes at **Pho (49)** **(£)** *(3 Great Titchfield St., 020-7436-0111, www.phocafe.co.uk; hours: M–Sa 12PM–10PM)* come from authentic recipes. Sleek, suave, seductive—that's **Hakkasan (50)** **(££-££££)** *(8 Hanway Pl., 020-7927-7000, www.hakkasan.com; hours: M–W 12PM–3:15PM, 6PM–11:15PM, Th–F 12PM–3:15PM, 6PM–12:15AM, Sa 12PM–4:15PM, 6PM–12:15PM, Su 12PM–4:15PM, 6PM–11:15PM)*, a London hot spot designed by Christian Liaigre. Chef Tong Chee Hwee prepares Chinese cuisine and *dim sum* to die for. From fish and chips to avocado with prawns and rainbow trout, **North Sea Fish Restaurant (45)** **(£-££)** *(7-8 Leigh St., 020-7387-5892, www.northseafishrestaurant. co.uk; hours: M–Sa 12PM–2:30PM, 5:30PM–11PM)* is one of the most famous seafood joints in London.

BARS & NIGHTLIFE:

The **Shochu Lounge** *(at Roka, see page 129, www.shochu lounge.com; hours: M–F 12PM–12AM, Sa 5:30PM–12AM, Su 5:30PM–10:30PM)* rates high for coolness; soft chairs, snazzy upholstery, and deep-toned wood make it warm and intimate, and the Japanese cocktails are delicious. The **Fitzroy Tavern (51)** *(16 Charlotte St., 020-7580-3714; hours: M–Sa 12PM–11PM, Su 12PM–10:30PM)*, famous watering hole of London's

bohemian literati between the two world wars, has a "Writers and Artists Bar" in the basement and pictures of its illustrious former patrons.

The Social (52) *(5 Little Portland St., 020-7636-4992, www.thesocial.com; hours: M–W 12PM–12AM, Th–Sa 12PM–1AM)* combines great DJs, hot music, and a lively crowd. Post-Victorian, pre-Modern, the **Duke (of York) (53)** *(7 Roger St., 020-7242-7230, www.dukepub.co.uk; hours: M–Sa 12PM–11PM, Su 12PM–10:30PM)* is a quirky pub that gives a taste of a London long past; it's rather hidden, so be persistent. **The Lamb (54)** *(94 Lamb's Conduit St., 020-7405-0713, www.youngs.co.uk; hours: M–W 12PM–11PM, Th–Sa 12PM–12AM, Su 12PM–10:30PM)* is outfitted with incredible Victorian "snob screens," etched-glass partitions that turn to hide the drinker.

WHERE TO SHOP

Target Gallery (55) *(7 Windmill St., 020-7636-6295)* specializes in modern British furniture, ceramics, glass, and textiles from the 1930s to the 1970s, as well as graphics, jewelry, and ornaments. Arts and crafts inspired by the early 20th-century movements find an outlet at **Contemporary Applied Arts (56)** *(2 Percy St., 020-7436-2344, www.caa.org.uk; hours: M–Sa 10AM–6PM)*. The quintessential London accessory, the "brollie," has been masterfully crafted by **James Smith & Sons Umbrellas (57)** *(53 New Oxford St., 020-7836-4731, www.james-smith.co.uk; hours: M–F 10AM–6PM, Sa 10AM–5:30PM)* since 1830; a Smith remains the finest of the species. **Museum Street (58)**, across from the British Museum, specializes in antique art, prints, and books.

Abbott and Holder *(30 Museum St., 020-7637-3981, www.abbottandholder-thelist.co.uk; M–Sa 9:30AM–6PM, Th til 7PM)* aims to make its oil paintings, watercolors, drawings, and prints affordable to as many people as possible, keeping prices in the £100 to £5000 range. Three floors of stationery and artist's supplies at the flagship store of **Paperchase (59)** *(213-215 Tottenham Court Rd., 020-7467-6200, www.paperchase.co.uk; hours: M–F 8:30AM–8PM, Sa 9AM–7PM, Su 12PM–6PM)* also sells great, inexpensive gift items.

WHERE TO STAY

Designed by Ian Schrager and Philippe Starck, **The Sanderson (60) (£££–££££)** *(50 Berners St., 020-7300-1400, www.morganshotelgroup.com)* is quirky and cool, a flight of fancy incorporating incongruous elements in surprising ways and playing on varying levels of transparency. Its restaurant, **Suka**, offering Malaysian cuisine, is super-chic, super-eclectic, and super-expensive. The hotel's other delight is the spa **Agua**. The **Charlotte Street Hotel (61) (£££–££££)** *(15 Charlotte St., 020-7806-2000, www.charlottestreethotel.com)* is charming and quietly elegant; its artwork and textiles reflect the Bloomsbury Group and Omega Workshop.

The Academy (62) (££) *(21 Gower St., 020-7631-4115, www.theetoncollection.com)* offers comfortable, charming rooms in a Bloomsbury town house. Hospitality and friendliness inhabit the **Morgan Hotel (63) (££)** *(24 Bloomsbury St., 020-7636-3735, www.morganhotel.co.uk)*, with small, well-appointed rooms. A cheap sleep, **Celtic Hotel (64)** (£) *(62 Guilford St., 020-7837-6737/9258, www.stmargarets hotel.co.uk)* is quiet, comfortable, and centrally located; but there's no elevator, and some rooms share baths. The luxurious **Hotel Russell (65)** (££) *(1-8 Russell Sq., 020-7837-6470, www.londonrussellhotel.co.uk, discounted rates online)* has been beautifully restored—one of its highlights being the building's marvelous mosaic floor, which had been covered up due to war damage. Visitors won't be disappointed with its comfortable rooms and convenient location.

chapter 6

KING'S CROSS

ISLINGTON

CLERKENWELL & SMITHFIELD

HOLBORN

KING'S CROSS
ISLINGTON
CLERKENWELL & SMITHFIELD
HOLBORN

Places to See:

1. St. Pancras International Station
2. Camley Street Natural Park
3. British Library
4. London Canal Museum
13. Almeida Theatre
14. Crafts Council Gallery
15. Screen on the Green Cinema
16. King's Head Theatre
17. Little Angel Theatre
39. Charterhouse
40. St. Etheldreda
41. Smithfield Market
42. Cloth Fair
43. St. Bartholomew-the-Great
44. St. Botolph's, Aldersgate
45. Postman's Park
46. Sadler's Wells
47. Museum of the Order of St. John
67. Lincoln's Inn
68. Lincoln's Inn Fields
69. Gray's Inn
70. Staple Inn
71. Old Curiosity Shop
72. Law Society
73. Royal Courts of Justice
74. Temple Bar Memorial
75. Middle Temple Hall
76. Inner Temple Hall
77. Temple Church
78. Dr. Johnson's House
79. Sir John Soane's Museum
80. St. Brides

Places to Eat & Drink:

5. St. Pancras Grand Brasserie
6. Camino
7. B@1
8. Egg
18. Frederick's
19. Afghan Kitchen
20. Rodizio Rico
21. Masala Zone
22. Ottolenghi Café
23. The Elk in the Woods
24. The Crown
25. The Old Queen's Head
26. The King's Head
27. Ladybird Bar
28. 69 Colebrooke Row

Where to Shop:

Where to Stay:

KING'S CROSS

 *King's Cross-St. Pancras*

● SNAPSHOT ●

When Neil Jordan shot his film *Mona Lisa* in King's Cross, the neighborhood was notorious for junkies and prostitutes, and known more as a train station in a dodgy area than a true neighborhood. But times change, and King's Cross is undergoing gentrification, including the opening of the high-speed Channel Tunnel Rail Link, named "High Speed 1," *(www.lcrhq.co.uk, 020-7391-4300)* to Paris (2 hrs. 15 min.) and Brussels (less than 2 hrs.) from St. Pancras International Station. Though parts of the district are still quite seedy and rough (better not to venture there alone at night), it is rapidly expanding, with hip clubs, shops, and loft development turning the gritty wasteland of warehouses into a stylish destination. Already, interesting restaurants are becoming part of the new landscape, though with the neighborhood still in transition, bars and clubs are more notable than restaurants. And at King's Cross train station (Euston Rd.), check out "Platform 9¾"—you just might bump into Harry Potter rushing to catch the train to Hogwarts.

PLACES TO SEE
Landmarks:

The marvelous glass and iron train shed of **St. Pancras International Station (1)** *(Euston Rd., 020-7843-7688, http://stpancras.com; hours: station 24/7, reception daily*

7AM–11PM) is a spectacular Victorian structure. The exterior is just as spectacular: a gingerbread Gothic in red brick, elaborately designed and detailed. The building above the ground-floor station was designed in 1874 by George Gilbert Scott as the Midland Grand Hotel. The **Camley Street Natural Park (2)** *(12 Camley St., 020-7833-2311, www.wildlondon.org.uk; hours: Oct–Mar Su–F 10AM–4:30PM, Apr–Sep Su–F 10AM–5:30PM)*, with ponds, marshes, woods, and meadows, is run by the London Wildlife Trust as a reserve for butterflies, insects, birds, and wildfowl, as well as nature-loving humans.

Arts & Entertainment:

In an uninspired exterior, the **British Library (3)** *(96 Euston Rd., switchboard: 0843-208-1144, www.bl.uk; Reading Rooms, hours: M 10AM–8PM, Tu–Th 9:30AM–8PM, F–Sa 9:30AM–5PM; Exhibition Galleries & Shop, M, W–F 9:30AM–6PM, Tu 9:30AM–8PM, Sa 9:30AM–5PM, Su 11AM–5PM)* contains a wealth of books (over 16 million), manuscripts, maps, and a world-class Sound Archive. Rare books and manuscripts include Shakespeare's First Folio and signature, King George III's library, the Lindisfarne Gospels, and a Gutenberg Bible. The **London Canal Museum (4)** *(12-13 New Wharf Rd., 020-7713-0836, www.canalmuseum.org.uk; hours: Tu–Su 10AM–4:30PM, first Th of each month 10AM–7:30PM)* is devoted to Carlo Gatti, who imported ice from Norway and stored it in the huge ice well visible in the museum's floor; it also displays canal equipment and depicts the life of canal workers.

PLACES TO EAT & DRINK
Where to Eat:

Stunningly elegant and romantic, **St. Pancras Grand Brasserie (5) (£–£££)** *(Grand Terrrace, St. Pancras International Station, 020-7870-9900, www.searcys.co.uk/stpancrasgrand; hours: Restaurant, M–Sa 7AM–11PM, Su 8AM–11PM; Champagne Bar, M–F 8AM–11PM, Sa 7AM–11PM, Su 9AM–10:30PM)* is one of London's hottest eateries. **Camino (6) (£–££)** *(3 Varnisher's Yard, The Regent Quarter, 020-7841-7331, www.camino.uk.com; hours: Restaurant, M–F 12PM–3PM, 6PM–11PM, Sa 12PM–4PM, 6PM–11PM, Su 12PM–4PM; Bar, M–W 12PM–12AM, Th–Sa 12PM–1AM, Su 12PM–11PM)* offers tapas in the bar; the Spanish menu in the restaurant includes great grilled food.

Bars & Nightlife:

B@1 (7) *(33 Caledonian Rd., 020-7837-5652, www.beatone.co.uk; hours: Su–W 4:30PM–12AM, Th–Sa 4:30PM–2AM)* boasts good music, friendly people, and a cool decor, especially the spectacular Verner Panton chandelier. The fashionistas have started pouring into **Egg (8)** *(200 York Way, 020-7871-7111, www.egglondon.net; F 10PM–8AM, Sa 10PM–11AM, last admission Su at 6AM)*, known for its dance music as well as its fabulous garden and roof terraces.

WHERE TO SHOP

After working with Jimmy Choo, **Joe Tan (9)** *(98 Caledonian Rd., 020-7837-3835)* went on to design shoes for Princess Diana and other celebrities. His King's Cross boutique offers ready-made footwear, with his signature exquisite detailing. **Housmans (10)** *(5 Caledonian Rd., 020-7837-4473, www. housmans.com; hours: M–F 10AM–6:30PM, Sa 10AM–6PM, Su 12PM–6PM)* is a purveyor of radical books and periodicals. They also sell a wide range of stationery and T-shirts. **St. Pancras International Station (1)** *(see page 137)* is home to a plethora of shops.

WHERE TO STAY

Pullman London St. Pancras (11) (£££) *(100-110 Euston Rd., 020-7666-9000, www.accorhotels.com)* offers modern businesslike comfort but little Old World charm. London rooftop views from the higher floors are a plus. **Premier Travel Inn King's Cross (12) (££)** *(26-30 York Way, 0871-527-8672, www.premiertravelinn.com)* offers inexpensive motor lodge-type accommodations.

> There's something about doing theater in London—it sinks a little bit deeper into your soul as an actor.
>
> —*Christian Slater*

ISLINGTON

⊖ *Angel, Highbury & Islington*

● SNAPSHOT ●

People left the City in droves after the Plague (1665) and the Great Fire (1666). Nearby Islington soon became a fashionable suburb of the wealthy while the poor settled into tenements on its outskirts, in Finsbury and Moorfields. By the early 19th century, however, the rich had moved out, leaving Islington to decline into poverty. Though George Orwell, Evelyn Waugh, and Joe Orton lived there in the 20th century, it wasn't until the 1970s that the area was restored and artists, writers, and bankers moved in. Renovated Georgian houses and Victorian terraces mark the stately elegance of this upper-middle-class neighborhood, while the dilapidation around the fringe gives it a certain edge. Full of boutiques and bars, fashionable Islington also teems with theaters, making it popular with actors and theatergoers and assuring the neighborhood retains energy and vibrancy. Chain stores are increasingly commercializing Upper Street, while Islington's old edginess can still be found in the shops, bars, and eateries of Essex Road.

PLACES TO SEE
Arts & Entertainment:

The award-winning **Almeida Theatre (13)** (*Almeida St., 020-7359-4404, www.almeida.co.uk; hours: performance days, M–Sa 10AM–11:30PM; non-performance days, M–Sa*

10AM–6PM) collaborates with exceptional theater and film actors (such as Claire Bloom, Juliette Binoche, Ralph Fiennes, and Kevin Spacey) and first-rate directors (Sir Richard Eyre and Howard Davies, among others). The **Crafts Council Gallery (14)** *(44a Pentonville Rd., 020-7806-2500, www.craftscouncil.org.uk; call for hours)* houses a collection of over 1200 contemporary British crafts, promoting decorative and applied arts, and supporting the work of British craftspeople. **Screen on the Green Cinema (15)** *(83 Upper St., 0871-906-9060, www.screencinemas.co.uk; call for showtimes)* shows indies and mainstream movies. Many plays at the **King's Head Theatre (16)** *(115 Upper St., info: 020-7226-8561, box office: 020-7478-0160, www.kingshead theatre.org; call for showtimes)* go on to West End runs. **Little Angel Theatre (17)** *(14 Dagmar Passage, off Cross St., 020-7226-1787, www.littleangeltheatre.com; call for showtimes)* performs all sorts of puppet shows.

PLACES TO EAT & DRINK
Where to Eat:
Frederick's (18) (££-£££) *(106 Camden Passage, 020-7359-2888, www.fredericks.co.uk; hours: M–Sa 12PM–2:30PM, 5:45PM–11PM)* is wonderfully airy, elegant, and romantic; the Modern British-European fare hits the spot. **Afghan Kitchen (19) (£)** *(35 Islington Green, 020-7359-8019; hours: Tu–Sa 12PM–3:30PM, 5:30PM–11PM)*, a tiny café, offers traditional Afghan curries. Visit Brazilian **Rodizio Rico (20) (££-£)** *(77–78 Upper St., 020-7354-1076, www.rodiziorico.com; hours M–Th 5:30PM–11:30PM, F–Sa 12PM–12AM, Su 12PM–11PM)* for all-you-can-eat salads and barbecued meat. For great

value on Indian food dine at **Masala Zone (21) (£)** *(80 Upper St., 020-7359-3399, www.masalazone.com; hours: M–F 12:30PM–3PM, 5:30PM–11PM, Sa 12:30PM–11PM, Su 12:30PM–10:30PM)*. A local favorite, **Ottolenghi Café (22) (£-££)** *(287 Upper St., 020-7288-1454, www. ottolenghi.co.uk; hours: M–Sa 8AM–11PM, Su 9AM–7PM)* serves succulent Middle Eastern-Mediterranean dishes; the decor is unexotically minimalist, but shared tables encourage friendliness.

Bars & Nightlife:

The Elk in the Woods (23) *(39 Camden Passage, 020-7226-3535, www.the-elk-in-the-woods.co.uk; hours: M–F 8:30AM–11PM, Sa 10:30AM–11PM, Su 10:30AM–10:30PM)*, with its log-cabin-style interior, is a warm, friendly bar. **The Crown (24)** *(116 Cloudesley Rd., 020-7837-7107, www.crownislington.co.uk; hours: M–Sa 12PM–11PM, Su 12PM–10:30PM)* is a quiet, calm gastropub. Once an Elizabethan pub, **The Old Queen's Head (25)** *(44 Essex Rd., 020-7354-9993, www.theold queenshead.com; hours: Su–W 12PM–12AM, Th 12PM–1AM, F–Sa 12PM–2AM)* was rebuilt in 1829, retaining the original ceiling and chimneypiece.

A theater in a pub, **The King's Head (26)** *(115 Upper St., 020-7226-4443, www.kingsheadtheatre.pub.co.uk; hours: M–W 12PM–1AM, Th–Sa 12PM–2AM, Su 12PM–12:30AM)* serves up ale along with vaudeville, Irish music, and individual performers. For large cocktails and eclectic music stop at the **Ladybird Bar (27)** *(70 Upper St., 207-359-1710, Su–Th 5PM–2AM, F–Sa 5PM–4AM)*. **69 Colebrook Row (28)** *(69 Colebrook Row, 07-540-528593, 69colebrookerow.com;*

hours: Su–W 5PM–12AM, Th 5PM–1AM, F–Sa 5PM–2AM),
the "bar with no name," serves interesting cocktails with
'20s-style music. Classic cocktails abound in saloon-style
Wenlock & Essex (29) *(18-26 Essex Rd, 020-7704-0871,
www.wenlockandessex.com, hours: M–Th, Su 10:30AM–
12PM, F–Sa 10:30AM–2AM)*. Soul jazz is king at
Electrowerkz (30) *(7 Torrens St., 020-7837-6419, call for
hours)*, with reggae/ska/jazz-funk every other Saturday.

WHERE TO SHOP

Although **Upper Street**, Islington's main drag, has been
heavily commercialized, people still flock here from all
over the world for the theaters, bars, restaurants, and
shops. At **twentytwentyone (31)** *(274 Upper St., 020-7288-
1996, www.twentytwentyone.com; hours: M–Sa 10AM–
6PM, Su 11AM–5PM)* designer furniture and homewares
are often limited-edition pieces. **Diverse (32)** *(294 Upper
St., 020-7359-8877, www.diverseclothing.com; hours:
M–Sa 10:30AM–6:30PM, Th til 7PM, Su 11:30AM–
5:30PM)* stocks cutting-edge designer creations, including
Hussein Chalayan and Martin Margiela; Kate Moss and
Dido are regular customers. Kids' clothing and toys at
Igloo (33) *(300 Upper St., 020-7354-7300, www.igloo
kids.co.uk; hours: M–W 10AM–6:30PM, Th 10AM–7PM,
F–Sa 9:30AM–6:30PM, Su 11AM–5:30PM)* are irresistible.

Camden Passage (34) *(www.camdenpassageislington.co.uk)* is
famous for the antiques market held on Wednesdays
(7AM–3PM) and Saturdays *(8AM–4PM)*. Besides regular
antiques shops, **Camden Passage (34)** and its extension
Islington High Street (35) feature several charming arcades of
dealers' stalls: **The Mall Arcade** *(359 Islington High St.)* is full

of treasures big and small; others are **Gateway** *(Camden Passage)*, **Pierrepont** *(Camden Passage)*, **Fleamarket** *(7 Pierrepont Row)*, and **Angel Arcades** *(118 Islington High St.)*, as well as **The African Waistcoat Company** *(33 Islington Green, 020-7704-9698, www.africanwaistcoatcompany.com)*. **Annie's** *(12 Camden Passage, 020-7359-0796, www.annies vintageclothing.co.uk; hours: daily 11AM–6PM)* has wonderful vintage clothing and beaded flapper dresses; and the **Tadema Gallery** *(10 Charlton Pl., Camden Passage, 020-7359-1055, www.tademagallery.com; call for hours)* specializes in exquisite late-19th- and early-20th-century jewelry (Art Nouveau, Jugendstil, British Arts & Crafts, Art Deco). **Rockarchive Gallery** *(110 Islington High St., 020-7704-0598, www.rockarchive.com; hours: M–Sa 11AM–6PM, Su 11AM–5PM)* focuses on rare rock and roll photos and related books, posters, and postcards.

Cross Street (36) is full of interesting shops. **Fandango** *(2 Cross St., 079-7965-0805, www.fandango.uk.com; hours: W–Sa 11AM–6PM or by appt.)* carries mid-20th-century objects for the home. **Cross Street Gallery** *(40 Cross St., 020-7226-8600, www.artforsale.co.uk)* showcases contemporary paintings and prints.

WHERE TO STAY

Spacious, comfortable rooms at the **Hilton Islington (37)** *(£-££) (53 Upper St., 020-7354-7700, www.hilton.com/islington)* are equipped with high-speed Internet access. Though generic in style, **Jury's Inn Islington (38)** *(£-££) (60 Pentonville Rd., 020-7282-5500, londonhotels.jurysinns.com)* offers large rooms, modern facilities, and comfort.

⊖ *Angel, Farringdon, Barbican,*
St. Paul's, Chancery Lane

● **SNAPSHOT** ●

Trendy Clerkenwell saw a conversion of warehouses into stylish lofts in the 1990s as Islington's desirability factor expanded southward. Clerkenwell, the medieval name of the district, means "the clerks' well"—an old well where medieval parish clerks performed plays. The neighborhood is riddled with medieval wells, remnants of the Fleet River that once ran through the area. Today's watering holes—hip bars and restaurants—decidedly cater more to fashionistas than monastics. Clerkenwell and Smithfield, to the south, are a mecca for young, cutting-edge designers and their followers.

PLACES TO SEE
Landmarks:

In 1611 **Charterhouse (39)** *(Sutton's Hospital, Charterhouse Sq., 020-7253-9503, www.thecharterhouse.org; guided tours M–Sa by appt)* was converted from the Carthusian monastery outlawed by Henry VIII to a hospital for the elderly poor and a charity school. The 14th-century chapel, cloisters, and a 17th-century library still exist.

Step inside **St. Etheldreda (40)** *(14 Ely Pl., 020-7405-1061, www.stetheldreda.com; hours: M–Sa 8AM–5PM, Su 8AM–12:30PM)*, Britain's oldest Catholic church and the only 13th-century Gothic building that survived the Great Fire of 1665, and feel like you've stepped back in time; the stained-glass windows are superb. **Smithfield Market (41)** *(Charterhouse St.)*, or **London Central Meat Market**, began trading in livestock in the 12th century. Now a meat market, it was built by Victorian architect Horace Jones in 1868. Much of it was destroyed in the blitz and later rebuilt. Stroll down picturesque **Cloth Fair (42)**, a street named after the medieval and Elizabethan textile fair. Note the 17th-century houses at Nos. 41 and 42, with their lovely bay windows.

St. Bartholomew-the-Great (43) *(West Cloth Fair, 020-7248-2294, www.greatstbarts. com; hours: M–F 8:30AM–5PM/mid-Nov–mid-Feb til 4PM, Sa 10:30AM–4PM, Su 8:30AM–8PM)*, one of London's oldest parish churches, dates from the early-12th century. It is believed that Rahere, a courtier of Henry I, founded the church in extreme gratitude after a miraculous recovery from malaria, which he attributed to St. Bartholomew. Parts of the church have been rebuilt over the centuries; the interior is Elizabethan. It was a film location for *Shakespeare in Love* and *Four Weddings and a Funeral*. **St. Botolph's, Aldersgate (44)** *(Aldersgate St., 020-7606-0684; Tu & Th only, call for hours)* has a staid Georgian exterior and an exuberant interior. Its churchyard was transformed in 1880 into **Postman's Park (45)** *(King Edward St.)*, where the Victorian painter G. F. Watts created a poignant memorial to honor acts of bravery by ordinary people. Beautiful

William Morris-style plaques on one wall tell their stories. One plaque reads: *Soloman Galaman: Aged 11, died of injuries September 6, 1901 after saving his little brother from being run over in Commercial Street: "Mother, I saved him but I could not save myself."*

ARTS & ENTERTAINMENT:

One of the world's most important classical ballet and contemporary dance venues, **Sadler's Wells (46)** *(Rosebery Ave., info: 020-7863-8198, box office: 0844-412-4300, www.sadlerswells.com; hours: box office M–Sa 10AM–8PM)* hosts outstanding companies, including Pina Bausch, Matthew Bourne, William Forsythe, American Ballet Theatre, Rambert Dance Company, and Birmingham Royal Ballet, among others. The **Museum of the Order of St. John (47)** *(St. John's Gate, St. John's Lane, 020-7324-4005, www.museumstjohn.org.uk; hours: M–Sa 10AM–5PM)* presents the history of the Order of Hospitaller Knights, from medieval Christian medics in the Crusades to today's ambulance service providers.

PLACES TO EAT & DRINK
Where to Eat:

Exmouth Market (48) is full of trendy restaurants, bars, and shops; the old Monday morning market still brims with food stalls. The North African and Spanish dishes at **Moro (££-£££)** *(34-36 Exmouth Mkt., 020-7833-8336, www.moro.co.uk; hours: M–Sa 12PM–2:30PM, 6PM–10PM, Su 12:30PM–2:45PM, tapas all day at bar M–Sa 12PM–10PM)* are fantastic; such a hit with the glitterati, it's rather hard to get a table. Once a butcher's shop, **Medcalf (£-£££)** *(40 Exmouth Mkt., 020-7833-3553, www.medcalfbar.co.uk;*

kitchen hours: M–Th 12PM–3PM, 6PM–9:45PM, F–Sa 12PM–3PM, 6PM–10:20PM, Su 12PM–4PM; bar open M–Th, Sa, til 11PM, F til 12AM) drums up hearty British food. **Cottons (£-££)** *(70 Exmouth Mkt., 020-7833-3332, www.cottons-restaurant.co.uk; hours: daily 12PM–11:30PM)* offers excellent Caribbean food and a friendly atmosphere.

The Michelin-starred **St. John Bar & Restaurant (49) (££-£££)** *(26 St. John St., 020-3301-8069, www.stjohngroup.uk.com; hours: Restaurant: M–F 12PM–3PM, 6PM–11PM, Sa 6PM–11PM, Su 1PM–3PM; Bar: M–F 11AM–11PM, Sa 6PM–11PM, Su noon–5PM)* recalls its previous existence as a smokehouse and has an appropriately meat-oriented menu, from duck breast to braised veal to pot roast. The bar is amazing, with skylights soaring 20 feet above the customers. A cozy eatery, **Pho (£)** *(86 St. John St., 020-7253-7624, www.phocafe.co.uk; hours: M–F 12PM–3PM, 6PM–10PM, Sa 6PM–10:30PM)* offers authentic Vietnamese food. Good food that won't break the bank—that's **Little Bay (50) (£)** *(171 Farringdon Rd., 020-7278-1234, www.littlebay.co.uk; hours: M–Sa 12PM–12AM, Su 12PM–11PM)*, where the electrical-wire-and-marbles chandelier vies with gargoyles for kitsch award of the year. From fish and chips to lobster and Cornish crab, **The Brasserie on St. John Street (51) (£-££)** *(360-362 St. John St., 020-7837-1199, www.the-brasserie.com; hours: Tu–Sa 12PM–3PM, 5:30PM–11PM, Su 12PM–8PM when Sadler's Wells has a performance)* offers a wide selection of fish and seafood. **Smiths of Smithfield (52) (££-£££)** *(67-77 Charterhouse St., 020-7251-7950, www.smithsofsmithfield.co.uk; hours: opens M–F 12PM–3PM, 6PM–11PM, Sa 6PM–11PM)*, another great British chophouse, adds Thai and Italian flavoring to rare traditional British food, like Gloucester Old Spot pork fillet with bok choy; the more informal second-floor dining room is less expensive **(£-££)**; and the ground-floor bar serves snacks and breakfast.

The Eagle (53) (£-££) *(159 Farringdon Rd., 020-7837-1353; hours: M–Sa 12PM–11PM, Su 12PM–5PM)* was  reputedly the pub that started the "gastropub" movement— pubs serving great food at reasonable prices—with its first-rate Mediterranean-British mix in a warm, casual setting. Another excellent gastropub, **The Coach & Horses (54) (£-££)** *(26-28 Ray St., 020-7278-8990, www.thecoachandhorses.com; hours: M–F 12PM–11PM, Sa 6PM–11PM, Su 1PM–5PM)* offers innovative dishes, like potato gnocchi with rabbit ragu or miso-braised pork belly; but beware, service is slow. **Vivat Bacchus (86) (£-£££)** *(47 Farringdon St., 020-7353-2648, www.vivatbacchus.co.uk; hours: M–F 12PM–late, food til 10:30PM, drinks til 11:30PM)* prides itself on its creative Modern European cuisine, great wine cellar, and huge variety of cheeses.

Bars & Nightlife:

Superclub **Fabric (55)** *(77a Charterhouse St., 020-7336-8898, www.fabriclondon.com; hours: open F 10PM, Sa–Su 11PM)* has four dance floors and superstar DJs. **Scala (56)** *(275 Pentonville Rd., 020-7833-2022, www.scala-london.co.uk; call for hours & showtimes)*, a club with four floors and three bars, hosts live music and performances.

Sprawl on a sofa at **Raduno (57)** *(85 Charterhouse St., 020-7253-8941, www.raduno.co.uk; call for hours)* and sip its stupendous cocktails; the dance space is on the third floor. If what you want is a tiny, charming pub, head for the **Jerusalem Tavern (58)** *(55 Britton St., 020-7490-4281, www.stpetersbrewery.co.uk/london; hours: M–F 11AM–11PM)*. Built in 1546, lovely **Ye Olde Mitre Tavern (59)** *(1 Ely Pl., Ely Court, 020-7405-4751, yeoldemitreholburn.co.uk; hours: M–F 11AM–11PM)* still has a cherry tree where Queen Elizabeth I allegedly danced on May Day.

WHERE TO SHOP

Designers Harriet Wallace-Jones and Emma Sewell opened Wallace Sewell (60) *(24 Lloyd Baker St., corner of Amwell St., 020-7833-2995, www.wallacesewell.com; hours: Tu–F 10:30AM–5:30PM, Sa 11AM–6PM)* to show-case their woven scarves, throws, and cushions (also sold at Liberty, the Crafts Council, and abroad). Several jew-elry shops in **Exmouth Market (48)** *(see page 148)* are notable. Over 40 jewelry designers are featured at **EC One** *(41 Exmouth Mkt., 020-7713-6185, www.econe.co.uk; hours: M–W, F 10AM–6PM, Th 11AM–7PM, Sa 10:30AM–6PM)*, while handmade jewelry, shoes, belts, and scarves are among the delights at **Family Tree** *(53 Exmouth Mkt., 020-7278-1084, www.familytreeshop.co.uk; hours: M–Sa 11AM–6PM)*. The street-smart designs of Antoni & Alison (61) *(43 Rosebery Ave., 020-7833-2141, www.antoni andalison.co.uk; hours: M–F 10:30AM–6:30PM, Sa*

12:30PM–5:30PM) go beyond their original photo print T-shirts. The fabulous creations of over 100 top jewelry and textile designers are on display at **Lesley Craze Gallery (62)** *(33-35a Clerkenwell Green, 020-7608-0393, www.lesleycrazegallery.co.uk; hours: Tu–F 10:30AM–6PM, Th til 7PM, Sa 11AM–5:30PM).*

WHERE TO STAY

Striking architecture and design at **The Zetter (63) (££-£££)** *(86-88 Clerkenwell Rd., 020-7324-4444, www.thezetter.com)* are retro-modern in this converted Victorian warehouse; rooms encircle the atrium, while the ground floor bar and restaurant are quirky and modern yet cozy. Romantic and full of antiques, **The Rookery (64) (££-£££)** *(12 Peter's Ln., Cowcross St., 020-7336-0931, www.rookeryhotel.com)* is a delightful Victorian town house hotel; its large period bed-rooms and glass-covered garden exude charm and personality. The top floor suite, "Rook's Nest," has spectacular views of London. **Malmaison (65) (£-££)** *(18-21 Charterhouse Sq., 0845-365-4247, www.malmaison.com)*, a hotel chain, has large modern rooms, Internet, and a gym in a Victorian building on a picturesque square. **Citadines Barbican (66) (£-££)** *(7-21 Goswell Rd., 020-7566-8000, www.citadines.com)* offers comfortable though uninspired apartments.

HOLBORN

🚇 *Holborn, Chancery Lane, Temple, Blackfriars*

• SNAPSHOT •

Holborn is synonymous with law courts and journalism. The Royal Courts of Justice and the four Inns of Court—the law societies and barristers' offices—were established here; and Fleet Street was where all the great newspapers resided until the 1980s. The verdant squares and gardens of the Inns add to the area's calm, dignified atmosphere. The famous Silver Vaults are also located here.

PLACES TO SEE
Landmarks:

Parts of **Lincoln's Inn (67)** *(Lincoln's Inn Fields and Serle St., 020-7405-1393, www.lincolnsinn.org.uk; hours: grounds M–F 7AM–7PM; chapel M–F 12PM–2:30PM; guided tours by appt. 10:30AM & 2:30PM),* one of the four Inns of Court, date from the 15th century. Its architectural styles cover numerous historical eras: Gothic, Tudor, Palladian. Among its famous alumni were Oliver Cromwell, John Donne, and William Penn. Across the street, **Lincoln's Inn Fields (68)** is the biggest public square in London. A public execution site under the Tudors and Stuarts, it is now a protected public park. **Gray's Inn (69)** *(Gray's Inn Rd., 020-7458-7800, www.graysinn.info; call for hours)* dates from the 14th century. Shakespeare's *A Comedy of Errors* was first performed in this legal center and law school in 1594. In the 19th century, Charles Dickens worked there as a law clerk.

153

In the 16th century wool was weighed and taxed at spectacular **Staple Inn (70)** *(High Holborn)*, one of the few extant Tudor buildings in London.

The 17th-century **Old Curiosity Shop (71)** *(13-14 Portsmouth St., 020-7405-9891, www.curiosityuk.com; hours: M–Sa 10:30AM–7PM)* is said to be London's oldest shop and the one on which Charles Dickens's novel was based. The architectural highlight of the **Law Society (72)** *(113 Chancery Ln., 020-7242-1222, www.lawsociety.org.uk; call for hours)* is the northern annex by Charles Holden, the Arts and Crafts designer responsible for many London Tube stations.

The **Royal Courts of Justice (73)** *(Strand, 020-7947-7684, www.courtservice.gov.uk; hours: M–F 9AM–4:30PM)* are England's main civil courts. Its beautiful Gothic architecture is worth a visit. The building has 1,000 rooms and 3.5 miles of hallways. Visitors can sit in on current trials, and admission is free. In the evening, it becomes a fabulous event venue. Outside the law courts, **Temple Bar Memorial (74)** *(Fleet St.)*, once a gate, now the statue of a griffin, marks the boundary between the City of London and Westminster. **Fleet Street** itself is synonymous with journalism. The first newspaper, *The Daily Courant*, set up shop here in 1702; others soon followed. Today, only Reuters and the Press Association remain here.

Middle Temple and **Inner Temple**, the other two Inns of Court (besides Lincoln's and Gray's inns), get their name from the Knights Templar, once based here. Gaslit after sundown, the warren of courtyards gives the area a medieval village atmosphere. With a stunning Elizabethan interior, **Middle**

Temple Hall (75) *(Middle Temple Ln., 020-7427-4800, www.middletemple.org.uk; hours: M–F 10AM–4PM)*, built in 1573, is graced by a large table, a gift from Elizabeth I. In 1601 Shakespeare's *Twelfth Night* was performed there. Tours of **Inner Temple Hall (76)** *(King's Bench Walk, 020-7797-8250, www.innertemple.org.uk; call for hours)* and other buildings can be booked *(020-7797-8211)*. It is believed that the Knights Templar were initiated in the crypt of the 12th-century **Temple Church (77)** *(King's Bench Walk, 020-7353-3470, www.templechurch.com; call for hours)*, in whose nave lie ten 10th- to 13th-century effigies of Knights Templar. Scenes from the novel *The Da Vinci Code* are set here. The church is architecturally important in that it is the city's only round church. Enter **Dr. Johnson's House (78)** *(17 Gough Sq., 020-7353-3745, www.drjohnsonshouse.org; hours: May–Sept M–Sa 11AM–5:30PM, Oct–Apr M–Sa 11AM–5PM)* and you enter the 18th century. The essayist Samuel Johnson, who resided here from 1749 to 1759, wrote the first English dictionary, published in 1755. Not always enthused with his work, his dictionary defines the word "dull" as "to make dictionaries is *dull* work."

Arts & Entertainment:

Sir John Soane's Museum (79) *(13 Lincoln's Inn Fields, 020-7405-2107, www.soane.org; hours: Tu–Sa 10AM–5PM, first Tu of month, special evening opening 6PM–9PM)* comprises the home and vast collections of the 19th-century architect who designed the Bank of England. A fabulous house, with all manner of architectural tricks and details, from unfolding panels to a glass dome bringing light into the basement, it's a fascinating, surprising place. Christopher Wren

designed **St. Brides (80)** *(Fleet St., 020-7427-0133, www.stbrides.com; hours: M–F 8AM–6PM, Sa call for hours, Su 10AM–6:30PM)*, whose octagonal layered spire is supposed to have inspired the design of tiered wedding cakes. Due to its Fleet Street location, the church is known as the "journalists' church," with many journalists' weddings and memorials still held here.

PLACES TO EAT & DRINK
Where to Eat:

Fantastic New French cuisine makes **Pearl (81)** *(££-££££)* *(Renaissance Chancery Court Hotel, 252 High Holborn, 020-7829-7000, www.pearl-restaurant.com; hours: breakfast M–F 6:30AM–11AM, Sa–Su 7AM–12PM, restaurant daily 12PM–10PM, bar daily 12PM–1AM)* a huge hit; the Scandinavian-inspired decor is very cool. Get a taste of world-class Korean BBQ and cuisine at **Asadal (82)** *(£-££)* *(227 High Holborn, 020-7430-9006, www.asadal.co.uk; hours: M–Sa 12PM–3PM, 6PM–11PM, Su 6PM–10:30PM)*. A favorite dish among the regulars is their handmade mandoo (dumplings). At **The Chancery (84)** *(££-£££)* *(9 Cursitor St., 020-7831-4000, www.thechancery.co.uk; hours: M–F 12PM–2:30PM, 6PM–10PM, Sa 6PM–10PM)* creative Modern European cuisine, floor-to-ceiling windows, and friendly staff make it a hit. The **Gaucho Chancery (85)** *(££-££££)* *(125 Chancery Ln., 020-7242-7727, www.gauchorestaurants.co.uk; hours: M–F 12PM–11PM, Sa 5PM–11PM)* may be a chain eatery, but the steak is a meat lover's delight. Samuel Johnson, Charles Dickens, and Mark Twain frequented the pub **Ye Olde Cheshire Cheese (87)** *(£-££)* *(145 Fleet St., 020-7353-6170; hours: M–F food 12PM–10PM, pub 11AM–11PM, Sa food 12PM–2:30PM,*

6PM–9:30PM, pub 12PM–11PM); today you can get good pub food in its fabulous maze of atmospheric rooms.

Bars & Nightlife:

Ye Olde Cock Tavern (88) *(22 Fleet St., 020-7353-8570, www.taylor-walker.co.uk; hours: M–W 7AM–12AM, Th 7AM–1AM, F 7AM–2AM, Sa 12PM–9PM)*, Fleet Street's oldest pub, was a favorite with Dr. Johnson, Samuel Pepys, Charles Dickens, and T. S. Eliot. Another Fleet Street bar is the 17th-century **Old Bell Tavern (83)** *(95 Fleet St., 020-7583-0216; hours: M–Th 10AM–11:30PM, F 10AM–12AM, Sa 12PM–6PM)*. The 1667 **Cittie of York (89)** *(22-23 High Holborn, 020-7242-7670; M–Sa 12PM–11PM)* is a charming hoot: the front room gives onto a church's nave at the back, confessionals and all—just in case you go overboard on the ale.

WHERE TO SHOP

Once safes for the wealthy, the London Silver Vaults (90) *(53-64 Chancery Ln., 020-7242-3844, www.thesilvervaults.com; hours: M–F 9AM–5:30PM, Sa 9AM–1PM)* house over 30 dealers in the world's largest antique silver market (dinner services, silverware, jewelry, and baubles).

WHERE TO STAY

A landmark Edwardian building with marble staircase, Chancery Court Hotel (91) (££–£££) *(252 High Holborn, 020-7829-9888, www.chancerycourthotel.com, www.renaissance hotels.com)* has appeared in the films *Howards End* and *The Saint*. This sumptuous hotel features lofty archways, plush rooms, and luxurious marble bathrooms. Citadines Covent Garden/Holborn (92) (££–£££) *(94-99 High Holborn, 020-7395-8800, www.citadines.com)* offers studios and one-bedroom flats with kitchenettes.

chapter 7

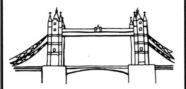

HOXTON & SHOREDITCH

EAST END: SPITALFIELDS &
WHITECHAPEL

CITY

HOXTON & SHOREDITCH
EAST END: SPITALFIELDS & WHITECHAPEL
CITY

Places to See:

1. Hoxton Square
2. Columbia Road Flower Market
3. Geffrye Museum
4. Iniva
5. dreambagsjaguarshoes
6. Comedy Café
28. Spitalfields Market
29. Dennis Severs' House
30. Christ Church, Spitalfields
31. Jamme Masjid Mosque
32. Brick Lane
33. Whitechapel Bell Foundry
34. Whitechapel Art Gallery
35. Old Truman Brewery
36. Electric Blue Gallery
56. ST. PAUL'S CATHEDRAL ★
57. St. Mary-le-Bow
58. St. Stephen Walbrook
59. Old Bailey
60. St. Giles, Cripplegate
61. Whitbread's Brewery
62. Broadgate Centre
63. Liverpool Street Train Station
64. Lloyd's of London

65. 30 St. Mary Axe
66. The Monument
67. St. Magnus the Martyr
68. All Hallows by the Tower
69. TOWER OF LONDON ★
70. TOWER BRIDGE ★
71. Barbican Centre
72. Museum of London
73. Guildhall Art Gallery
74. Bank of England Museum

Places to Eat & Drink:

1. Hoxton Square
   Bluu Bar
   Hoxton Square Bar and Kitchen
   Zigfrid Von Underbelly
7. Brick Lane Beigel Bake
8. Albion
9. Rivington Bar and Grill
10. Cantaloupe
11. Eyre Brothers
12. The Book Club
13. Fifteen
14. Boundary Restaurant & Rooftop
15. George & Dragon

★ *Top Pick*

Where to Shop:

Where to Stay:

HOXTON & SHOREDITCH

 *Old Street, Hoxton*

• SNAPSHOT •

In the mid-1990s young British artists, people like Tracey Emin and Damien Hirst, moved to the Hoxton wasteland, converting industrial spaces left abandoned since World War II into lofts and studios. Soon the area became what it is today: hip, trendy, bohemian. It retains its artistic character, with artists still living and working in many of the lofts; but with rents rising in Hoxton, emerging artists are looking for digs further away, toward Bethnal Green and Hackney. Hoxton and the area south of Old Street, Shoreditch, are dynamic neighborhoods, full of some of London's cutting-edge galleries, designers' shops, restaurants, bars, and clubs. Once neighboring villages, Hoxton and Shoreditch have had a colorful history. In 1598 playwright Ben Jonson killed actor Gabriel Spencer in a duel in Hoxton Fields, now known as Hoxton Square. In Victorian times, Shoreditch was packed with rowdy music halls.

PLACES TO SEE
Landmarks:

Hoxton Square (1) is the area's center, lined with some of the city's hippest restaurants, bars, and galleries. Though shops and galleries are open during the day, it's not until evening falls that the characters come out of the wood-work and the area's *anima* truly makes itself felt. On

Sundays the flamboyant, popular **Columbia Road Flower Market (2)** *(www.columbiaroad.info; Su 8AM–3PM)* is a fascinating swirl of colors, sounds, and scents. Flower sellers from Cockneys to West Indians hawk posies in performances worthy of old Shoreditch.

Arts & Entertainment:

The **Geffrye Museum (3)** *(136 Kingsland Rd., 020-7739-9893, www.geffrye-museum.org.uk; hours: Tu–Sa 10AM–5PM, Su 12PM–5PM)* is dedicated to English domestic interiors and gardens of the past 400 years, with period rooms re-created in chronological order. **Iniva (4)** *(1 Rivington Pl., 020-7729-9616, www.iniva.org; hours: exhibitions Tu–F 11AM–6PM, Th til 9PM, Sa 12PM–6PM; library Tu–F 10AM–1PM, 2PM–5PM)* presents outstanding solo and group exhibitions, often partnering with notable London museums such as the Tate, the ICA, and the Hayward Gallery as well as foreign institutions such as New York's New Museum of Contemporary Art. Its talks and symposia present fascinating debates on international art and culture. Bar and exhibition space **dreambagsjaguarshoes (5)** *(32-34 Kingsland Rd., 020-7729-5830, www.jaguarshoes. com; call for hours)* presents up-and-coming artists. **Comedy Café (6)** *(66-68 Rivington St., 020-7739-5706, www. comedycafetheatre.co.uk; call for hours)* is one of London's best stand-up comedy venues.

PLACES TO EAT & DRINK

Where to Eat:

Open 24 hours a day, **Brick Lane Beigel Bake (7) (£)** *(159 Brick Ln., 020-7729-0616; hours: 24/7)* is legendary for its "salt beef" bagels. Good, simple British food is what you get at **Albion (8)** (£–££) *(2-4 Boundary St., 020-7729-1051, albioncaff.co.uk; hours: M–Sa 8AM–11PM, Su 8AM–10:30PM)*, from sandwiches to Welsh rarebit, smoked mackerel, and Shepherd's pie. **Rivington Bar and Grill (9)** (££) *(28-30 Rivington St., 020-7729-7053, www.rivingtongrill.co.uk; hours: M–F 8AM–11AM, 12PM–11PM, Sa 11AM–4PM, 6PM–11PM, Su 11AM–4PM, bar menu all day every day)*, with its all-white interior, serves traditional British food. From loud music to trendy clientele, **Cantaloupe (10)** (£–££) *(35-42 Charlotte Rd., 020-7729-5566, www.cantaloupe.co.uk; hours: M–W 12PM–11PM, Th–Sa 12PM–12AM, Su 12PM–10:30PM)* and its Mediterranean menu fit the area's industrial-cool profile.

The **Eyre Brothers (11)** (££–£££) *(70 Leonard St., 020-7613-5346, www.eyrebrothers.co.uk; hours: M–F 12PM–3PM, 6:30PM–10:45PM, Sa 7PM–10:45PM)* gastropub centers its inventive menu on Spanish cuisine with accents of Mozambique; 1970s retro-decor, great wines, and good music make the place inviting. **The Book Club (12)** (£) *(100-106 Leonard St., 020-7684-8618, www.wearetbc.com; hours: M–W 8AM–12AM, Th–F 8AM–2AM, Sa 10AM–2AM, Su 10AM–12AM)* draws a younger crowd interested in mixing good, healthy food with cultural events and a lively bar, all in a reconverted Victorian warehouse. Jamie Oliver again scores high on hipness at **Fifteen (13)** (££–£££) *(15 Westland Pl., 020-3375-1515, www.fifteen.net; hours: daily 12PM–*

3PM, 6PM–10PM): Chefs, once disadvantaged kids, cook up Mediterranean dishes in the downstairs dining room and offer Italian in the upstairs trattoria. The French cuisine at **Boundary Restaurant & Rooftop (14) (££-££££)** *(2-4 Boundary St., entrance in Redchurch St., 020-7729-1051, www.theboundary.co.uk; hours: M–Sa 6:30PM–10:30PM, Su 12PM–4PM, bar M–Sa 6PM–12AM, Su 12PM–5PM)* includes classics such as frogs' legs and gruyere soufflé as well as delicacies such as *boeuf bordelaise* (steak filet in red wine sauce), *dodine de caille* (roast quail), *pot-au-feu de pigeon* (roast pigeon), or fish selections. A less expensive prix-fixe menu is available. Or try **Albion (8)**, downstairs.

Bars & Nightlife:

In and around **Hoxton Square (1)** there are many happening bars. Sleek and modern, with stainless steel fixtures, **Bluu Bar** *(1 Hoxton Sq., 020-7613-2793, www.bluu.co.uk; hours: daily 10AM–12AM)* has a reputation for DJs leaning toward drum 'n' bass dance tunes. Next door and partially underground, **Hoxton Square Bar and Kitchen** *(2-4 Hoxton Sq., 020-7613-0709, www.hoxtonsquarebar.com; hours: M 11AM–12AM, Tu–Th 11AM–1AM, F–Sa 11AM–2AM, Su 11AM–12:30AM)* is another local hangout. Sitting on a Chesterfield sofa at **Zigfrid Von Underbelly** *(11 Hoxton Sq., 020-7613-1988, www.zigfrid.com; hours: M–Th 12PM–1AM, F–Sa 12PM–3AM, Su 12PM–12:30AM)*, you can watch the world go by on the square. Kitschy decor forms the backdrop to trendy **George & Dragon (15)** *(2-4 Hackney*

Rd., 020-7012-1100; hours: daily 6PM–12AM), which features a mix of 70s/80s music and DJs. **Cargo (16)** *(83 Rivington St., 020-7739-3440, www.cargo-london.com; hours: M–Th 6PM–1AM, F–Sa 6PM–3AM, Su 6PM–12AM)* is a place to check out for its music, with world-famous DJs spinning and scratching. **Club Aquarium (17)** *(256-264 Old St., 020-7251-6136, www.clubaquarium.co.uk; call for hours)* lives up to its name with a swimming pool and Jacuzzi; the scene is lively.

WHERE TO SHOP

Shop at fashion-forward No-One (18) *(1 Kingsland Rd., 020-7613-5314, www.no-one.co.uk; hours: M–W, F–Sa 11AM–7PM, Th 11AM–8:30PM, Su 12PM–6PM)* for unisex fashion and accessories, and stop at the café next door for a break. Junky Styling (19) *(12 Dray Walk, Old Truman Brewery, 91 Brick Ln., 020-7247-1883, www.junkystyling.co.uk; hours: M–F 10:30AM–7PM, Sa–Su 11AM–7PM)* takes overstocked designer clothes and completely refashions them. Art publications at bookartbookshop (20) *(17 Pitfield St., 020-7608-1333, www.bookartbookshop.com; hours: W–F 1PM–7PM, Sa–Su 12PM–6PM)* include the cutting edge in creativity.

A gallery and bookshop, KK Outlet (21) *(42 Hoxton Sq., 020-7033-7680, www.kkoutlet.com; hours: M–F 9AM–6PM, Sa 12PM–5PM)* presents collaborative shows by contemporary international artists and offers books on communications and graphics hard to find elsewhere. The classic furniture, ceramics, and silverware at SCP (22) *(135-139 Curtain Rd., 020-7739-1869, www.scp.co.uk; hours: M–Sa 9:30AM–6PM, Su 11AM–5PM)* are from the finest modern and contemporary designers. Treacle (23) *(110-112 Columbia Rd., 020-7729-0538, www.treacleworld.com; hours: Sa 12PM–5PM, Su 9AM–4PM)* sells typical British desserts, tea paraphernalia, and 1950s ceramics. Hipsters and intellectuals interested in graphics descend on Kemistry (24) *(43 Charlotte Rd., 020-7729-3636, kemistrygallery.co.uk; hours: M–Sa 10AM–6PM)* for its hip, engaging exhibits of graphic designers. Funky Tatty Devine (25) *(236 Brick Lane, 020-7739-9191, www.tattydevine.com; hours: M–F 10AM–6:30PM, Sa 11AM–5PM, Su 10AM–5PM)* sells fun jewelry, arty T-shirts, shoes, and accessories.

WHERE TO STAY

Sleek, modern, and bold, with great city views, the Crowne Plaza London Shoreditch (26) **(££)** *(100 Shoreditch High St., 020-7613-9800, www.saintgregory hotel.co.uk)* is good for business travelers; but its swankiness feels like a veneer. Fairly generic, Express by Holiday Inn (27) **(£-££)** *(275 Old St., 020-7300-4300, www.hiexpress.com)* is clean and comfortable, with large rooms.

EAST END: SPITALFIELDS & WHITECHAPEL

⊖ Aldgate, Aldgate East, Shoreditch High Street

• SNAPSHOT •

East of Central London lie the areas of Spitalfields and Whitechapel, also known as the East End. Among the city's earliest suburbs, the East End soon became a point of arrival for people of other countries seeking refuge from persecution. French Huguenots, Germans, Irish, Jews, Eastern Europeans, and Bangladeshis have, over the centuries, given the area its multiethnic character. Non-white ethnic groups comprise more than half the population of today's Spitalfields and Whitechapel, creating a rich social fabric. The East End also has a thoroughly working-class history: factories, foundries, breweries, and tanneries provided jobs from late-medieval times to the 1950s. Not all the work was industrial, however: crime, gangs, prostitution, and child labor were rife. In the late-19th century, Jack the Ripper brutally murdered prostitutes in Whitechapel, and in 1911 the Sidney Street Siege became a shoot-out between police and an anarchist group.

With growing gentrification, many of the area's industrial buildings have been turned into upscale restaurants, cafés, and bars, especially around Spitalfields Market and Brick Lane. Massive renovation and development took place in preparation for the 2012 Olympics, including the new East London Line of the Underground. While the East End's multiethnic character continues to animate and enrich the area, its industrial and insalubrious past has already become the stuff of history books, novels, and period films.

PLACES TO SEE
Landmarks:

The area's centerpiece is the old **Spitalfields Market (28)** *(Commercial St., Lamb St./Brushfield St., www.spitalfields.co.uk; hours: Stalls: M–F 10AM–5PM, Su 9AM–5PM; Shops: daily 10AM–7PM)*, which began as a produce market in 1682 and now sells everything from organic veggies and beauty products to clothing, retro furniture, and CDs. The ten rooms of **Dennis Severs' House (29)** *(18 Folgate St., 020-7247-4013, www.dennis severshouse.co.uk; hours: Su 12PM–4PM, M 12PM–2PM, booking required for "Silent Night" tour M 6PM–9PM & Oct–Mar W 6PM–9PM)* re-create 18th- and 19th-century life in Spitalfields— what artist Severs called a "still-life drama." With broken bread on the plates and tea in the cups, it looks as if the inhabitants have only stepped away for a minute.

Nicholas Hawksmoor's 1729 **Christ Church, Spitalfields (30)** *(Commercial St./Fournier St., 020-7377-6793, www.christchurchspitalfields.org; hours: Tu 11AM–4PM, Su 1PM–4PM, M–F 11AM–4PM if venue not in use)*, with its splendid portico and soaring spire, was part of a plan to break the area's Protestant Huguenot stronghold, a threat to the Church of England. French Huguenots, fleeing religious persecution in 18th-century Catholic France, became silkweavers in **Fournier Street**; today Bengalis work the sewing machines. The area's multicultural history is encapsulated in the **Jamme Masjid Mosque (31)** *(59 Brick Ln., 020-7247-6052, www.bricklanejammemasjid.co.uk; call for hours)*: built as a Huguenot chapel in 1743, it served as a synagogue in the 19th century, a Methodist chapel in the early 1900s, and a mosque in 1976. **Brick Lane (32)**, named for the area's now-defunct brick factories, is London's main Bengali thoroughfare, full of curry restaurants, shops selling silks, spices, and foods, and a Sunday street market. It has become a hot nightspot, with funky bars and clubs popping up in converted factories. Since 1570 the **Whitechapel Bell Foundry (33)** *(32-34 Whitechapel Rd., 020-7247-2599, www.whitechapelbellfoundry.co.uk; hours: M–F 9AM–4PM)* has been casting bells, including Big Ben and Philadelphia's Liberty Bell.

Arts & Entertainment:

The **Whitechapel Art Gallery (34)** *(77-82 Whitechapel High St., 020-7522-7888, www.whitechapelgallery.org; hours: Tu–Su 11AM–6PM, Th til 9PM)* exhibits major contemporary artists. David Hockney's first exhibit opened here in 1970, and in the 1950s and 1960s shows included artists such as Robert Rauschenberg, Jackson Pollock, and Anthony Caro. The **Old Truman Brewery (35)** *(91-95 Brick Ln., 020-7770-6000, www.trumanbrewery.com)* hosts exhibits of emerging artists. In its studios and showrooms artists, photographers, fashion designers, graphic designers, and architects work and exhibit side by side. **Electric Blue Gallery (36)** *(64 Middlesex St., 020-7247-5370; hours: daily 11AM–8:30PM)* is an eclectic mix of artists and hip hairdressers, a surefire hot spot for anyone fascinated by design or media. While you're in the area, check out **Raven Row** *(56 Artillery Ln., 020-7377-4300, www.ravenrow.org; hours: W–Su 11AM–6PM)*, another popular, chic, hip gallery that mounts cutting-edge exhibitions.

PLACES TO EAT & DRINK
Where to Eat:

Brick Lane's curry eateries offer animated ambience but not London's finest Indian cuisine. However, one of the best is **Brick Lane Clipper (37) (£)** *(104 Brick Ln., 020-7377-0022, www.bricklaneclipper.com; hours: M–F 12PM–2:30PM, 5:30PM–12AM, Sa–Su 12PM–12AM)*: its good food is not the typical Indian fare. **Café 1001 (38) (£)** *(1 Dray Walk, 91 Brick Lane, 020-7247-6166, www.cafe1001.co.uk; hours: daily 6AM–12AM)* at **Old Truman Brewery (35)** *(see page 169)* has hot panini and smoothies. Warm and modern, **Canteen (39) (£-££)** *(2 Crispin Pl., 0845-686-1122, www.canteen.co.uk; hours: M–F 8AM–11PM, Sa 9AM–11PM, Su 9AM–10PM)* serves good updated British food, using seasonal produce. Relaxing, with an upscale menu, **The English Restaurant (40) (££-£££)** *(Spitalfields Mkt., 52 Brushfield St., 020-7247-4110, www.theenglishrestaurant.com; hours: M–F 8AM–11PM, Sa 9AM–11PM, Su 9AM–7PM)* serves modern versions of British dishes, turning them into works of art.

Bars & Nightlife:

The **Ten Bells (41)** *(84 Commercial St., 075-3049-2986, www.tenbells.com; hours: daily 11AM–11PM)* is the mid-18th-century pub believed to have been frequented by many of Jack the Ripper's victims. With good DJs and a wide variety of live music, **Vibe Bar (42)** *(Old Truman Brewery, 91-95 Brick Ln., 020-7247-3479, www.vibe-bar.co.uk; hours: Su–Th 11AM–11:30PM, F–Sa 11AM–late)* is a trendy club. Another popular music nightspot is **Big Chill Bar (43)** *(91-95 Dray Walk/Brick Ln., 020-7392-9180, www.bigchill.net; hours: Su–W 12PM–12AM, Th–Sa 12PM–1AM)*. One of the Truman Brewery's hippest locales is **93 Feet East (44)** *(150 Brick Ln., 020-7770-6006, www.93feeteast.co.uk; call for hours)*; exposed beams, chandeliers, drapes, a slick bar, and top-notch live music and club nights make it a happening place. Elegant, with wood paneling and Victorian decor, the **Golden Heart (45)** *(110 Commercial St., 020-7247-2158; hours: M–Sa 11AM–11PM, Su 12PM–10:30PM)* is the pub choice of artists. More in keeping with the quarter's working class aura, **Pride of Spitalfields (46)** *(3 Heneage St., 020-7247-8933; hours: M–Sa 11AM–11PM, Su 12PM–10:30PM)* is a traditional East End pub.

WHERE TO SHOP

The market in **Petticoat Lane (47)** *(Middlesex St.)* got its name from the Sunday clothing bazaar (leather coats top the list) held there. Prudish Victorians renamed the road Middlesex Street, but the old name prevailed. **Spitalfields Market (28)** *(see page 168; hours: stalls M–F 10AM–5PM, Su 9AM–5PM, shops daily 10AM–7PM)* has become famous for trend-setting fashions, furniture, antiques, and food; Thursday is the Antiques Market, while Sunday is bustling. At the Spitalfields Arts Market (48) *(Market St., Spitalfields Market, www.spitalfields.co.uk; hours: Mar–Oct 1st Th–Su of month, Apr & Jun also 2nd Th–Su, Nov–Christmas every Th–Su, see web site for details; closed Jan–Feb)* you can buy original works directly from the artists.

Check out @ Work (49) *(156 Brick Ln., 020-7377-0597, www.atworkgallery.co.uk; hours: M–Sa 11AM–6PM, Su 12:30PM–5:30PM)* for eye-catching jewelry designs. This Shop Rocks (50) *(129-131 Brick Ln., 020-7739-7667, hours: daily 11AM–6PM)* carries high-end women's vintage clothing. Rokit (51) *(101 & 107 Brick Ln., 020-7375-3864/020-7247-3777, www.rokit.co.uk; hours: M–F 11AM–7PM, Sa–Su 10AM–7PM)* is known for vintage clothing and its own label. Cheshire Street (52) is lined with shops selling homewares, most open only on weekends. Though Story (53) *(4 Wilkes St., 020-7377-0313, home btconnect.com/story)* looks like a gallery, it carries vintage clothing, unique furniture, and natural bath products. Visit The Laden Showroom (54) *(103 Brick Ln., 020-7247-2431, hours daily 11AM–6:30PM)* for fashion from independent designers. Fabulous gourmet food store Verde & Co. (55) *(40 Brushfield St., 020-7247-1924, verde andco.co.uk)*, owned by writer Jeanette Winterson, makes an art of fresh fruits and vegetables.

WHERE TO STAY

While exploring the East End is fascinating, it's best to stay in hotels in nearby Clerkenwell, the City, or elsewhere in London.

CITY

⊖ *Blackfriars, St. Paul's, Bank, Mansion House, Cannon Street, Monument, Tower Hill, Aldgate, Liverpool Street, Moorgate*

● SNAPSHOT ●

The City—officially the City of London, also nicknamed the Square Mile—is the area originally settled by the Romans from the first century B.C. to the fifth century A.D. Londinium, as they called it, was enclosed by a stone wall, parts of which are still visible along the street London Wall. Anglo-Saxons followed Romans, then were sacked by Vikings. After the Norman Conquest of 1066, the City underwent serious development. William the Conqueror built the first castle along the Thames, the Tower of London, and traders and merchants amassed enormous wealth. They formed the London Guilds and other institutions still important to the City. But the Square Mile has also suffered significant losses: it was nearly completely destroyed by the Great Plague of 1665 and the Great Fire of 1666. It recovered by rebuilding in stone and brick, with architects such as Sir Christopher Wren recruited to plan the city's reconstruction and transform it into a modern capital. St. Paul's Cathedral, a plethora of churches, and powerful bank-

ing institutions are constant reminders of the Square Mile's rebirth.

Today the City is London's financial center, the heart of one of the world's largest economies, and home to an influential stock exchange. Yet for all its modernity, it retains a sense of its history, from its bridges to its pubs, its churches to its markets. This is where Spenser and Chaucer were born, where Shakespeare thrived, and where the famous, infamous, and less notable stood trial at the Old Bailey—characters such as William Penn, Oscar Wilde, and the Kray gangster brothers.

PLACES TO SEE
Landmarks:

TOP PICK!

Many historic buildings, livery companies (guilds), and churches stand alongside modern architecture of steel and glass in the City. Undoubtedly the most famous is ★ST. PAUL'S CATHEDRAL (56) *(Ludgate Hill, 020-7246-8357, www.stpauls.co.uk; hours: M–Sa 8:30AM–4PM)*, designed by Sir Christopher Wren. A soaring, grand edifice built

from 1675 to 1708 on the ashes of the Great Fire, it survived the blitz of World War II and became a symbol of the resilience of Londoners and their city. Spectacular inside and out, the cathedral's West Front, with its colonnades, pediment, and towers, is surpassed in grandeur only by the imposing dome, second largest in the world after St. Peter's in Rome. The nave and transepts are breathtaking; but don't miss the Golden Gallery, with spectacular views of London, and the Whispering Gallery, both in the dome. The crypt contains tombs and memorials to famous people, including Wren himself, Reynolds, Turner, Lord Nelson, Lawrence of Arabia, Henry Moore, and Gilbert and Sullivan. **London Walks** *(020-7624-3978, www.walks.com)* offers tours of Wren's churches, including **St. Paul's Cathedral (56)**, **St. Mary-le-Bow (57)** *(Cheapside, 020-7248-5139, www.stmaryle bow.co.uk; hours: M–W 7:30AM–6PM, Th 7:30AM–6:30PM, F 7:30AM–4PM, Sa–Su usually closed, call for info)* and **St. Stephen Walbrook (58)** *(39 Walbrook, 020-7626-9000, ststephenwalbrook.net; hours: M–F 10AM–4PM)*. A London tradition claims only people born within earshot of the bells of St. Mary-le-Bow can be called Cockneys.

Another City landmark, less spiritual, is the Central Criminal Court, known as the **Old Bailey (59)** *(corner of Newgate St. and Old Bailey, 020-7248-3277, www.old baileyonline.org; hours: public galleries: M–F 10AM–1PM, 2PM–5PM)*. It was built in 1907 on the site of the 1539 session house of the insalubrious Newgate Prison. Famous defendants have stood in its witness box, where in 1895 Oscar Wilde gave his historic "love that dares not speak its name" speech. The 16th-century church **St. Giles, Cripplegate (60)** *(Fore St., 020-7638-1997, www.stgiles cripplegate.com; call for hours)* survived the Great Fire of 1666 only to be devastated in the blitz of World War II, leaving only the tower standing. The church where Oliver

Cromwell was married (1620) and John Milton buried (1674) was restored in the 1950s, an anomaly within the modern **Barbican** area, a conglomeration of high-rise apartments, shops, and an arts center.

Whitbread's Brewery (61) *(Chiswell St., not open to public)* is a well-preserved landmark of a major 18th-century industry. **Broadgate Centre (62)** *(Exchange Sq., 020-7505-4068, www.broadgate.co.uk)*, an office and shopping complex with an outdoor skating rink (a summer performance venue), looks over the restored, glass-roofed **Liverpool Street Train Station (63)** *(Liverpool St./Bishopsgate, 0845-711-4141, www.networkrail.co.uk/aspx/897.aspx, www.nationalrail.co.uk)*, a film location for *Mission: Impossible.*

The City skyline is etched by several notable modern buildings. **Lloyd's of London (64)** *(1 Lime St., 020-7327-1000, www.lloyds.com; not open to the public)* is housed in a 1986 building by Richard Rogers (architect, with Renzo Piano, of Paris's Pompidou Center), all high-tech and stainless steel, with ducts, pipes, elevator shafts, and other mechanical constructions on the outside. The **30 St. Mary Axe (65)** *(30 St. Mary Axe, www.30stmaryaxe.com)*, slyly dubbed the "Erotic Gherkin," is the 2003 Lord Norman Foster glass and steel marvel; cigar-shaped, with indoor atriums and gardens, it culminates in a glass dome.

In a memorial to the event that destroyed the City and was the catalyst for its renewal, **The Monument (66)** *(Monument St., at Fish St. Hill, 020-7626-2717, www.themonument.info; hours: Oct–Mar daily 9:30AM–*

5:30PM) commemorates the Great Fire of 1666. This Doric column is 202 feet high, the exact distance from the base of the column to the bakery in Pudding Lane where the fire began. The observation deck at the top offers breathtaking views of London. **St. Magnus the Martyr (67)** (*Lower Thames St., 020-7626-4481, www.stmagnus martyr.org.uk; hours: Tu–F 10AM–4PM*), built by Christopher Wren after the Great Fire, contains a model of the original London Bridge, demolished in 1758. Wren's pulpit and the organ case are worth a look. **All Hallows by the Tower (68)** (*Byward St., 020-7481-2928, www.allhallowsbythetower.org.uk; hours: M–F 8AM– 5PM, W til 6PM, Sa 10AM–4PM, Su 10AM–1PM*) was reconstructed after World War II on the foundations of the original seventh-century Saxon church. It contains a Saxon arch, Roman and Saxon relics, and a Crusader altar.

TOP PICK!

Steeped in the history of royal power, the ★**TOWER OF LONDON (69)** (*Tower Hill, 0844-482-7777, ticket office: 0844-482-7799, www.hrp.org.uk; hours: Mar–Oct Su–M 10AM–5:30PM, Tu–Sa 9AM–5:30PM, Nov–Feb Su–M 10AM–4:30PM, Tu–Sa 9AM–4:30PM*) has, over more than 900 years, been a royal palace, fortress, prison, and execution ground. The site of gruesome tortures and executions of traitors, the Tower is where two of Henry VIII's wives were beheaded. The two sons of Edward IV were imprisoned in the **Bloody Tower** by their uncle, Richard of Gloucester, in 1483 when their father died; Richard was crowned and the boy princes were never seen again. The highlights of the Tower are the **Crown Jewels**, the royal collection of crowns, scepters, orbs, and swords used in coronations and state celebrations; the **White Tower**, with its collection of armor and arms; and the **Chapel of St. John**, a lovely stone Romanesque chapel. Nearby is the wonderfully lavish ★**TOWER BRIDGE (70)** *(020-7403-3761, www.tower bridge.org.uk; hours: daily Apr–Sep 10AM–6PM, Oct–Mar 9:30AM–5:30PM)*, a Victorian feat of engineering and hydraulics. Designed by Sir John Wolfe Barry and Horace Jones, it has spanned the Thames since 1894. Two flamboyant towers stand in the middle of the river over the roadway; they are connected at the top by a catwalk, from which the city and river views are stupendous. Inside, the Tower Bridge Exhibition has interactive displays covering the bridge's history.

TOP PICK!

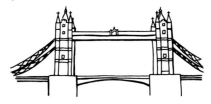

Arts & Entertainment:

Home to the London Symphony Orchestra, the **Barbican Centre (71)** *(Silk St., 020-7638-4141, box office: 020-7638-8891, www.barbican.org.uk; hours: M–Sa 9AM–*

11PM, Su 12PM–11PM) is a major arts venue housing a concert hall, two theaters, and a cinema. It presents top international artists of widely varied musical, theatrical, and dance genres. The **Museum of London (72)** *(150 London Wall, 020-7001-9844, www.museumoflondon. org.uk; daily 10AM–6PM)* re-creates London life from prehistoric times to the present through reconstructed streets and interiors, artifacts, and models.

The **Guildhall Art Gallery (73)** *(Guildhall Yard, off Gresham St., 020-7332-3700, www.cityoflondon.gov.uk; hours: M–Sa 10AM–5PM, Su 12PM–4PM)* houses portraits of politicians, a collection of pre-Raphaelites, works by Constable and Reynolds, and the largest painting in Britain, John Copley's *Siege of Gibraltar*, which covers two floors. The **Bank of England Museum (74)** *(Threadneedle St., entrance on Bartholomew Lane, 020-7601-5545, www.bankofengland.co.uk/museum; M–F 10AM–5PM)* has ancient coins, bank notes, minting machines, and dioramas of 18th-century political cartoons; visitors can hold a real gold bar. Free lunchtime recitals are held at **St. Mary-le-Bow (57)** *(1PM, call for info, see page 175)*.

PLACES TO EAT & DRINK
Where to Eat:

Fun and stylish, **Haz (75) (£-££)** *(9 Cutler St., 020-7929-7923, www.hazrestaurant.co.uk; call for hours)* is lavish with its Turkish *meze* and kebabs. In a former sherry warehouse, **The Don (76) (££-£££)** *(The Courtyard, 20 St. Swithins Ln., 020-7626-2606, www.thedonrestaurant.com; hours: M–F*

12PM–3PM, 6PM–10PM) offers modern European cuisine and a great wine list. For a quick pizza or reliable Italian eats, **Pizza Express (77) (£-££)** *(125 Alban Gate, London Wall, 020-7600-8880, www.pizzaexpress.com; hours: M–F 11:30AM–11PM, Sa 11:30AM–10PM, Su 11:30AM–8PM)* is a sure deal. **Rhodes 24 (78) (££-££££)** *(Tower 42, 24th Fl., 25 Old Broad St., Reservations 020-7877-7703, www.rhodes24. co.uk; hours: M–F 12PM–2:30PM, 6PM–9PM; entrance security is tight, call in advance)* is a fantastic rendition of traditional British cuisine by creative head Chef Adam Gray; it's in the City's tallest building, so the view is to die for.

Bars & Nightlife:

Marble surfaces, gold mosaics, and mirror-covered niches are part of the wonderful Art Nouveau appeal of **The Black Friar (79)** *(174 Queen Victoria St., 020-7236-5474; hours: M–Th 10AM–11:30PM, F–Sa 10AM–12AM, Su 10AM–11PM)*. The **Jamaica Wine House (80)** *(12 St. Michael's Alley, 020-7929-6972, www.jamaicawinehouse.co.uk; hours: M–F 11AM–11PM)*, London's first coffeehouse, has been around—rebuilt, of course—since before the Great Fire; it's a hit with bankers. Atop the City's tallest skyscraper, **Vertigo 42 (81)** *(Tower 42, 25 Old Broad St., 020-7877-7842, www.vertigo42. co.uk; hours: reservations only, M–F 12PM–4:30PM, 5PM–11PM, Sa 5PM–11PM; entrance security is tight, call in advance)* is a champagne bar with incredible views.

WHERE TO SHOP

As the City is primarily the financial district, there is not much shopping here. However, if you have time, check out Leadenhall Market (82) *(Whittington Ave. at Gracechurch St., 020-7332-1703, www.leadenhall market.co.uk; hours: M–F 10AM–5PM)*. Once known for fish, meat, and poultry, it is now also full of clothing and gift shops, restaurants, and pubs. The street market on Fridays *(10AM–4PM)* sells a variety of gourmet foods, cheeses, and baked goods.

WHERE TO STAY

Design maven Terence Conran renovated the splendid Andaz London (83) (££-£££) *(40 Liverpool St., 020-7961-1234, london.liverpoolstreet.andaz.com)*, a 19th-century railroad hotel, keeping its original architectural and decorative elements. Stunning contemporary art fills the lobby, and the rooms are elegantly modern. On the magnificent former premises of the Midland Bank (a listed building) Threadneedles (84) (£££-££££) *(5 Threadneedle St., 020-7657-8080, www.theetoncollection.co.uk)* melds elegant modern furnishings with the lobby's wood paneling, decorative columns, and fantastic stained-glass dome. The Apex City of London Hotel (85) (££-£££) *(1 Seething Ln., 020-7702-2020, www.apexhotels.co.uk)*, an upscale chain, offers comfort and pleasant surroundings. The Tower (86) (£-£££) *(St. Katharine's Way, 0871-376-9036, Int'l: 0845-305-8335, www.guoman.com)* provides bedrooms, suites, and apartments in contemporary style, with high-speed Internet access, a gym, and other conveniences.

chapter 8

SOUTH BANK

SOUTHWARK &
BERMONDSEY

SOUTH BANK
SOUTHWARK & BERMONDSEY

Places to See:

Places to Eat & Drink:

★ *Top Pick*

All the world's a stage and all the men and women merely players.

—from William Shakespeare's As You Like It

SOUTH BANK

 Waterloo, Southwark, Lambeth North

*Or cross the river from Temple, Embankment,
Charing Cross, or Westminster*

● SNAPSHOT ●

Across the Thames from Central London is South Bank.
World War II bombings damaged the factories and
wharves of the area, which lay in ruins until 1951, when
it became the site of the Festival of Britain. Royal Festival
Hall, the only remaining structure of that celebratory
event, became the centerpiece around which other arts
and cultural institutions arose during the 1960s and
1970s. Since then, the Southbank Centre arts complex
has been a focal point of British theater,
music, film, and art. The millennial cel-
ebrations brought an influx of energy
and development to the entire area,
making it one of the capital's major
attractions. The London Eye is the
world's tallest observation wheel and a
draw for tourists. The Queen's Walk, a
pedestrian riverbank walkway, provides marvelous views
of many of London's most celebrated sights, as do all the
boardwalks ("promenades") along the riverside from
Westminster Bridge to Southwark Cathedral. This is one
of the most delightful jaunts in the city.

PLACES TO SEE
Landmarks:

At the southern end of South Bank, **Lambeth Palace (1)** *(Lambeth Palace Rd., closed to the public)* is the London residence of the Archbishop of Canterbury, head of the Church of England. Its Tudor gatehouse is one of the riverside's notable sights. Created for the turn of the millennium celebrations, the hugely popular **London Eye (2)** *(Jubilee Gardens, info: 0800-093-0123, bookings: 0871-781-3000, book a day in advance, www.londoneye.com; hours: daily Sep–Mar 28 10AM–8:30PM, Mar 29–Apr 14 & Jun 28–Aug 31 10AM–9:30PM, Apr 15–Jun 27 10AM–9PM; May–Jun F–Sa til 9:30PM)* is London's "Ferris wheel" from which 32 glass pods hang. Each holds 25 people. As you twirl above the city at the edge of the Thames, the views are magnificent. The **Tate to Tate Boat Service** *(see page 194)* stops at the London Eye on its way between the Tate Britain and the Tate Modern.

Arts & Entertainment:

The exciting arts venues of the **Southbank Centre (3)** *(Belvedere Rd., info: 020-7960-4200, box office: 0844-875-0073, www.southbankcentre.co.uk; call for showtimes)* include Royal Festival Hall, Queen Elizabeth Hall, the Purcell Room, Hayward Gallery, and the Saison Poetry Library. **Royal Festival Hall**, **Queen Elizabeth Hall**, and the **Purcell Room** host concerts of classical, contemporary, and world music, dance performances, and poetry readings. The **Hayward Gallery** exhibits modern and contemporary art. Film lovers mustn't miss the British Film Institute's **BFI Southbank/National Film Theatre (4)** *(Belvedere Rd., South Bank, 020-7928-3232, www.bfi.org.uk; hours:*

Su–Th 11AM–11PM, F–Sa 11AM–11:30PM, call for showtimes), unsurpassed for its retrospectives, international movies, and film archives. Its program "Movie Magic" screens films for kids. The **National Theatre (5)** (*Upper Ground, South Bank, info: 020-7452-3400, box office: 020-7452-3000, www.nationaltheatre.org.uk; call for showtimes*) showcases innovative troupes and stages new playwrights as well as fresh approaches to classics. Theater lovers also won't want to miss **The Old Vic (6)** (*The Cut at Waterloo Rd., box office: 0844-871-7628, www.old victheatre.com; call for showtimes*), whose reputation as "the actors' theater" has been borne out by the caliber of actors who have appeared there: Laurence Olivier, John Gielgud, Ralph Richardson, Alec Guinness, Peter O'Toole, Maggie Smith, and Judi Dench, among others. Kevin Spacey is its current artistic director.

Located in **County Hall**, which was once the seat of London's government, is the **London Aquarium (8)** (*County Hall, Westminster Bridge Rd., 0871-663-1678, www.visitsealife. com/london; hours: M–Th 10AM–6PM, F–Su 10AM– 7PM*). A chilling horror chamber, the **London Dungeon (37)** (*Belvedere Rd. between London Eye (2) and London Aquarium (8), bookings: 0871-423-2240, www.the dungeons.com; hours: M–W, F 10AM–4:30PM, Th 11AM– 4:30PM, Sa–Su 10AM–5:30PM, holidays til 6:30PM*) uses actors and special effects to re-create scenes of death, leprosy, plague, torture, and other gruesome moments in British history. The **Florence Nightingale Museum (9)** (*2 Lambeth Palace Rd., 020-7620-0374, www.florence-nightingale.co.uk; hours: daily 10AM–5PM*) is dedicated to the famous nurse and her innovative health care advances. The

Garden Museum (10) *(Lambeth Palace Rd., 020-7401-8865, www.gardenmuseum.org.uk; hours: Su–F 10:30AM–5PM, Sa 10:30AM–4PM, closed 1st M of month)* covers the history of gardening in Britain. Its own garden is lovely. The Imperial War Museum (11) *(Lambeth Rd., 020-7416-5000, www.iwm.org.uk; hours: daily 10AM–5PM)* displays military machines, war-themed arts, and exhibits on the effects of war on the homefront.

PLACES TO EAT & DRINK
Where to Eat:

The view from the Oxo Tower Restaurant, Brasserie, and Bar (12) (£££–££££) *(Top floor, Oxo Tower Wharf, Barge House St., 020-7803-3888, www.harveynichols.com/oxo-tower-london; hours: M–F 12PM–2:30PM, 6PM–11PM, Sa 12PM–2:30PM, 5:30PM–11PM, Su 12PM–3PM, 6:30PM–10PM)* is amazing; the Asian-style food is less so. The less expensive Brasserie (££) *(hours: M–Sa 12PM–11PM, Su 12PM–10PM)* features live music in a fun setting. In a former coach-maker's shop, Baltic (13) (££) *(74 Blackfriars Rd., 020-7928-1111, www.balticrestaurant.co.uk; hours: M 5:30PM–11:15PM, Tu–Sa 12PM–3:30PM, 5:30PM–11:15PM, Su 12PM–10PM)* offers fine Eastern European cuisine; the place is elegant and the front bar is hot; Saturday lunch is reasonably priced (£). The award-winning chefs at the Anchor & Hope (14) (£–££) *(36 The Cut, 020-7928-9898; hours: M 6PM–10:30PM, Tu–Sa 12PM–2:30PM, 6PM–10:30PM, Su lunch 2PM, bar hours: M 5PM–11PM, Tu–Sa 11AM–11PM, Su 12:30PM–5PM)* have put this gastropub and its hearty dishes on the map; it's hip but doesn't take reservations, so go early. Tas Restaurant (15) (£–££) *(33 The Cut, 020-7928-2111, www.tasrestaurants.co.uk/thecut.html; hours: M–Sa 12PM–11:30PM, Su 12PM–*

10:30PM) is a find; its delicious Turkish fare mixes distinctive tastes. Zesty Cuban food at **Cubana (16) (£)** (*48 Lower Marsh, 020-7928-8778, www.cubana.co.uk; hours: M–Tu 12PM–12AM, W–Th 12PM–1AM, F 12PM–3AM, Sa 3PM–3AM, Su 3PM–10PM*) is matched by great cocktails. Live salsa and Latin music rock the restaurant Wednesday–Saturdays. Among the many good restaurants at Southbank Centre, **Ping Pong (17) (£)** (*Festival Terrace, Southbank Centre, Belvedere Rd., 020-7960-4160, www.pingpongdimsum. com; hours: M–Sa noon–12AM, Su noon–11PM*) offers dim sum in a cool setting. The choice of buns, dumplings, and sticky rice dishes is appetizing.

Bars & Nightlife:

The **White Hart (18)** (*29 Cornwall Rd., 020-7928-9190, www.thewhitehartwaterloo.co.uk; hours: Su–M 12PM–11PM, Tu–Sa 12PM–12AM*) has gathered a following in the gentrified back streets of South Bank. The **Fire Station (19)** (*150 Waterloo Rd., 020-7620-2226, www.thefirestationwaterloo. com; hours: M 9AM–11PM, Tu–Th 9AM–12AM, F–Sa 9AM–1AM, Su 11AM–10:30PM*) is a popular pub near Waterloo Station. Nurse a pint at the outdoor tables of the **Riverfront Bar & Restaurant (20)** (*BFI Southbank, Belvedere Rd., 020-7928-0808, www.riverfrontbarandkitchen.com; hours: M–Sa 9AM–11PM, Su 10AM–10:30PM*) while watching the sun set over the Thames.

WHERE TO SHOP

Discover designer creations at Oxo Tower (21) (*1st and 2nd floors, Barge House St.*) craft studios: clothing, accessories, jewelry, and textiles. Jeweler **Alan Vallis** (*Unit 209, Oxo Tower Wharf, 020-7261-9898, www.alanvallis-oxo.com;*

hours: Tu–Sa 11AM–6PM or by appt.), for example, combines metals, beads, and stones to create striking pieces. Besides its street market, Lower Marsh (22) is also lined with shops oozing nostalgia. **Radio Days** (87 Lower Marsh, 020-7928-0800, www.radiodaysvintage.co.uk; hours: M–Sa 10AM–6PM, F til 7PM, or by appt.) deals in household objects, especially from the 1920s and 1950s. **What the Butler Wore** (131 Lower Marsh, 020-7261-1353, www.whatthebutlerwore.co.uk; hours: M–Sa 11AM–6PM) features vintage clothing (specializing in '60s and '70s styles). **Gramex** (25 Lower Marsh, 020-7401-3830; hours: M–Sa 11AM–7PM) sells classical records and CDs. The Calder Bookshop (23) (51 The Cut, 020-7620-2900, calderbookshop.com) has a fine selection of literary works and hosts talks and poetry readings. The gallery and museum shops in the **Southbank Centre (3)** (see page 186) are also worth checking out.

WHERE TO STAY

Opposite the Houses of Parliament, **London Marriott Hotel County Hall (24) (££-£££)** (London County Hall, Westminster Bridge Rd., 020-7928-5200, www.marriotthotels.com) has an elegant exterior and lobby, breathtaking views, and comfortable though generic rooms. **Premier Inn London County Hall (25) (£-££)** (Belvedere Rd., South Bank, 0871-527-8648, www.premierinn.com) offers unexciting budget rooms next to the London Eye. The quirky **Mad Hatter Hotel (26) (£-££)** (3-7 Stamford St., 020-7401-9222, www.fullershotels.com) is conveniently located and has a friendly pub.

SOUTHWARK & BERMONDSEY

🚇 *London Bridge, Southwark, Borough*

● SNAPSHOT ●

From the Middle Ages to the 18th century, Southwark, across the river and beyond the City's puritanical jurisdiction, was a licentious neighborhood of brothels, gambling, and all sorts of illicit pleasures. It was governed by the Bishops of Winchester, whose coffers swelled from the taxes they imposed on local prostitutes, known as "Winchester Geese." In the 16th century, Shakespeare set up the Globe Theatre in Southwark; its bawdy character endured until the Industrial Revolution. In the 18th and 19th centuries, factories, warehouses, and docks took over the area. Ultimately, it became derelict, destroyed by bombs in World War II.

Recent redevelopment, however, has transformed Southwark into a popular destination for art, culture, and design. Its centerpiece, the Tate Modern, is a stunning showcase for modern art.  Nearby, Shakespeare's Globe was reconstructed near the site of the original playhouse. Together these two institutions have been largely responsible for the massive neighborhood renovation. Bankside, along the river, affords fantastic views of London and the Thames, as does Millennium Bridge, the pedestrian river crosswalk. Borough, the southern domain of Southwark, is known for a bustling market founded in the 13th century, while Bermondsey, to the east, has traded in its tea and coffee warehouses for fancy lofts, offices, and the Design Museum. The exciting cultural venues of Southwark, Bermondsey, and the South Bank have made this "other" side of the river a vibrant quarter and mecca for those who love art, culture, and cutting-edge design.

PLACES TO SEE
Landmarks:
Millennium Bridge (27) certainly qualifies as high design. This dramatic suspension bridge, a feat of architectural prowess, gleams with stainless-steel balustrades, winglike structures swirling over the water from St. Paul's to the Tate Modern. While St. Paul's was being built, its designer, Sir Christopher Wren, stayed in one of the picturesque 17th-century row houses along Cardinal's Wharf (28), named after Cardinal Wolsey, Bishop of Winchester in 1529. The site of Southwark Cathedral (29) *(London Bridge, Cathedral St., 020-7367-6700, www.southwark.anglican.org/cathedral; hours: M–F 8AM–6PM, Sa–Su 8:30AM–6PM)* has a history as old as that of Londinium. It has been home to a Roman building, a Saxon minster, an Augustinian priory, parish church St. Saviour, and, in 1905, a cathedral. Parts of the building date from the 12th century. John Harvard, founder of Harvard University, was baptized here in 1607. Check out the stained-glass window of some of Shakespeare's

characters, as well as the church's many wonderful Gothic details.

The **Golden Hinde (30)** (*Pickfords Wharf, Clink St., 020-7403-0123, www.goldenhinde.com; daily 10AM–5:30PM*) is a reconstruction of the ship Sir Francis Drake commandeered as the first Englishman to circumnavigate the globe. He became Vice-Admiral of the English fleet that defeated the Spanish Armada. The ship's "Living History Experiences" re-create daily life on board—costumes, food, and all. The **George Inn (31)** (*77 Borough High St., 020-7407-2056, www.nationaltrust.org.uk; hours: daily 11AM–11PM*) is the only remaining galleried coaching inn in London. A National Trust landmark, its oak beams, wood paneling, and lattice windows are throwbacks to the 17th century. Its 1797 clock was made when Parliament levied a 5-shilling tax on timepieces; people sold theirs and relied on public clocks until, months later, the act was repealed.

Arts & Entertainment:

The stunning modern art collection at the ★**TATE MODERN (32)** (*Bankside, 020-7887-8888, www.tate.org.uk/modern; hours: Su–Th 10AM–6PM, F–Sa 10AM–10PM*),

housed in a brilliantly converted power station, ranks among the best in the world. It houses international modern art created since 1900. The museum blends different media, artists, and time frames together by grouping the works by theme. There are four main themes displayed: "States of Flux" (primarily devoted to Cubism,

Futurism, and Vorticism), "Idea and Object" (showcasing Minimalism), "Material Gestures" (focusing on post-war Abstraction), and "Poetry and Dream" (highlighting Surrealism). The list of masters is seemingly endless. You'll find works by Picasso, Dalí, Duchamp, Pollock, Miró, Monet, Giacometti, Lichtenstein, Klee, Mondrian, Kandinsky, and Chagall. Don't miss the entire room devoted to Rothko or Rodin's famous sculpture *The Kiss*. The museum also hosts a number of film screenings, and music performances. The **Tate to Tate Boat Service** *(Thames Clippers, 020-7001-2222, www.thamesclippers.com; quays at Tate Modern, London Eye, Tate Britain, and other piers)*, with interior design by Damien Hirst, doubles as a fabulous 20-minute river cruise.

Shakespeare's Globe (33) *(21 New Globe Walk, Bankside, info: 020-7902-1400, box office: 020-7401-9919, www.shakespeares globe.com; call for hours)* is a reconstruction of the Bard's original Elizabethan theatre, down to the thatched roof and open-air stage, yard, and galleries. The **Bankside Gallery (34)** *(48 Hopton St., 020-7928-7521, www.banksidegallery.com; hours: daily 11AM–6PM during exhibitions)*, home to the Royal Watercolour Society and the Royal Society of Painter-Printmakers, mounts temporary exhibitions. The wine "museum" **Vinopolis (35)** *(1 Bank End, info: M–F 020-7940-8300, Sa–Su 020-7940-8301, ext. 4031 or 2088, www.vinopolis.co.uk; hours: W 6PM–9:30PM, Th–F 2PM–*

9:30PM, Sa 12PM–9:30PM, Su 12PM–4PM, last entry 2 hrs before closing) takes visitors on a tour of the history of wine-making; it offers tastings, classes, and a wine shop.

On the site of the notorious Clink jail, the **Clink Prison Museum (36)** *(1 Clink St., 020-7403-0900, www.clink.co.uk; hours: Oct–Jun M–F 10AM–6PM, Sa–Su 10AM–7:30PM, Jul–Sep daily 10AM–9PM)* traces the history of imprisonment and torture of prostitutes, debtors, and thieves. Instruments of torture and "clinking" chains are displayed. For a view of what surgery was like before anesthetics or antiseptics, check out the **Old Operating Theatre (38)** *(9a St. Thomas St., 020-7188-2679, recorded info 020-8806-4325, www.thegarret.org.uk; hours: daily 10:30AM–5PM)*, a women's operating amphitheater where students watched from stands around a wooden table, and a box of sawdust collected dripping blood.

The **Unicorn Theatre (39)** *(147 Tooley St., 020-7645-0560, www.unicorntheatre.com; call for showtimes)* produces professional theater for children. The **HMS Belfast (40)** *(Morgan's Ln., Tooley St., 020-7940-6300, www.iwm.org.uk; hours: daily Mar–Oct 10AM–6PM, Nov–Feb 10AM–5PM)*, last of Europe's World War II battleships, has displays portraying wartime life aboard ship, with sounds, lights, and smells adding atmosphere. The **Design Museum (41)** *(Shad Thames, 020-7403-6933/020-7940-8790, www.designmuseum.org; hours: daily 10AM–5:45PM)* presents exciting exhibits ranging from graphics to product design. Fashion designer Zandra Rhodes and architect Ricardo Legorreta created the **Fashion and Textile Museum (42)** *(83 Bermondsey St., 020-7407-8664, www.ftmlondon.org; hours: Tu–Sa 11AM–6PM during exhibitions)*, a strikingly colorful building dedicated to British and international fashion since the 1950s. The **White Cube Gallery (43)** *(48 Hoxton Sq., 020-7930-5373, www.whitecube.com; hours: Tu–Sa 10AM–6PM)* exhibits top contemporary British artists—Lucian Freud, Nan Goldin, Tracey Emin, Damien Hirst, among others. Its openings are packed with international celebrities.

PLACES TO EAT & DRINK
Where to Eat:

You get good café food and river views at the **Tate Modern Café (£)** *(Tate Modern, level 1, Bankside/Sumner St., 020-7401-5014, www.tate.org.uk; hours: M–Th 10AM–6PM, F 10AM–9PM, Sa 9AM–7PM, Su 9AM–6PM)*; the Tate's top-floor restaurant has superb views but the food's mediocre. **Nando's (44) (£)** *(225–227 Clink St., 020-7357-8662, www.nandos. co.uk; hours: Su–Th 11:30AM–11PM, F–Sa 11:30AM–12AM)*, a great cheap eat, does fabulous Portuguese flame-grilled peri-peri chicken.

Vinopolis (35) *(see page 194)* boasts several good restaurants and bars. Although the wine's the star at **Cantina Vinopolis (££)** *(1 Bank End, 020-7940-8333, www. cantinavinopolis.com; hours: M–Th 12PM–3PM, 6PM–11:30PM, F–Sa 12PM–11:30PM)*, the Mediterranean food is quite good. **Brew Wharf Bar and Restaurant (£–££)** *(Stoney St., 020-7378-6601, www.brewwharf.com; hours: M–F 12PM–3PM, 5:30PM–11PM, Sa 12PM–11PM)* specializes in beer and Northern European dishes, like cassoulet and rotisserie chicken. **Wine Wharf (£–££)** *(Stoney St., Borough Mkt., 020-7940-8335, www.winewharf.com; hours: M–F 12PM–3PM, 5:30PM–11PM, Sa 12PM–11PM)* is another wine bar next door to Vinopolis that serves good food and over 400 varieties of wine.

Magdalen (45) (£–££) *(152 Tooley St., 020-7403-1342, www.magdalenrestaurant.co.uk; hours: M–F 12PM–2:30PM, 6:30PM–10PM, Sa 6:30PM–10PM)* is a find: good European menu, reasonably priced. Try the spicy gingerbread ice cream for dessert. **Delfina (46) (£–££)** *(50 Bermondsey St., 020-7564-2400, www.thedelfina.co.uk; hours: drinks: M–F 8AM–5PM; restaurant: M–Th 8AM–11:30AM, 12PM–3PM, F 8AM–11:30AM, 12PM–3PM, 7PM–10PM)*, a café in a warehouse converted into artists' studios, combines fabulous Mediterranean food with attractive art exhibits. Among other converted warehouse-lofts, the row of restaurants in the **Butlers Wharf Building (47)** *(Shad Thames)* has a gorgeous view of the City and the Tower of London. They include: Italian fare at **Cantina del Ponte (£–££)** *(36c Shad Thames, 020-7403-5403, www.cantinadelponte.co.uk; hours: M–Sa 12PM–3PM, 6PM–11PM, Su 12PM–3PM, 6PM–10PM)*; French-style seafood at upscale **Le Pont de la Tour (££–££££)** *(36d Shad Thames, 020-7403-8403, www.lepontdela tour.co.uk; hours: M–F 12PM–3PM, 6PM–11PM, Sa 12PM–4PM, 6PM–11PM, Su 12PM–4PM, 6PM–10PM)*; and traditional British meat and potatoes at **Butlers Wharf Chop House (££–£££)** *(36e Shad Thames, 020-7403-3403, www.chophouse-restaurant.co.uk; hours: M–F 12PM–3PM, 6PM–11PM, Sa 12PM–4PM, 6PM–11PM, Su 12PM–4PM, 6PM–10PM)*. Designer Terence Conran also had a hand in the **Blueprint Café (48) (££–£££)** *(Design Museum, 28 Shad Thames, 020-7378-7031, www.blueprintcafe.co.uk; hours: M–Sa 12PM–3PM, 6PM–11PM, Su 12PM–4PM)*, notable for its modern Europen cuisine and great river views. For innovative Italian cuisine, **Tentazioni (49) (££–£££)** *(2 Mill St., Lloyds Wharf, 020-7237-1100, www.tentazioni.co.uk; hours: Sa 6:30PM–10:45PM, M–F 12PM–2:45PM, 6:30PM–10:45PM)* is exquisite.

Bars & Nightlife:

Bars at the **Vinopolis (35)** include the **Brew Wharf** *(see page 196)*, the **Wine Wharf** *(see page 197)*, and **Bar Blue** *(1 Bank End, 020-7940-8333, www.barbluevinopolis.com; hours: M–W 12PM–3PM, 5PM–11PM, Th–Sa 12PM–11PM, Su 12PM–4PM)*, a glass-and-steel design enhanced by blue accents the color of Bombay Sapphire Gin. **Anchor Bankside (50)** *(34 Park St., 020-7407-1577; hours: M–W 11AM–11PM, Th–Sa 11AM–12AM, Su 12PM–11PM)* was the setting for a scene in *Mission: Impossible*; it was from here, over three centuries ago, that Samuel Pepys watched London burn in the Great Fire of 1666. Dickens was a regular at the **George Inn (31)** *(see page 193)*, a cozy historic pub of great character; its yard hosts actors and morris dancers who entertain patrons in the summer.

WHERE TO SHOP

The art bookshop at the **Tate Modern (32)** *(see page 193)* is the largest in Europe. Across the street, Marcus Campbell Art Books (51) *(43 Holland St., 020-7261-0111, www.marcuscampbell.co.uk; hours: M–Sa 10:30AM–6:30PM, Su 12PM–6PM)* specializes in rare and out-of-print books on late-20th-century art and artists. Before the crack of dawn on Fridays, antiques dealers are peddling their desirable wares at Bermondsey Market (52) *(Long Ln. & Bermondsey St., Bermondsey Sq., www.bermondseysquare.co.uk/ antiques.html; hours: F 4AM–1PM)*; the legendary early hours may come from an old law that allowed fencing of stolen goods before dawn in Bermondsey. For gourmet food, fruits, and vegetables, head for lively Borough Market (53) *(8 Southwark St., 020-7407-1002, www.borough market.org.uk; hours: Th 11AM–5PM, F 12PM–6PM, Sa 8AM–5PM)*; probably London's oldest food market, its archives date back to 1014.

WHERE TO STAY

London Bridge Hotel (54) (££-£££) *(8-18 London Bridge St., 020-7855-2200, www.londonbridgehotel.com)* provides elegant comfort and excellent service. Sleek and modern, the Ibis Styles London Southwark Rose Hotel (55) (££-£££) *(47 Southwark Bridge Rd., 020-7015-1480, ibisstyleshotel.ibis.com)* combines style with business facilities. Express by Holiday Inn Southwark (56) (£-££) *(103-109 Southwark St., 020-7401-2525, www.ichotels group.com)* is convenient and comfortable with up-to-date facilities. Mercure London Bridge Hotel (57) (££-£££) *(71-79 Southwark St., 020-7660 0683, www.mercure.com)* offers business chic, modern rooms, and a pleasant bar and restaurant.

chapter 9

NEAR LONDON

Places to See:
1. Camden Town
2. Canary Wharf
3. Wimbledon
4. Kew Gardens
5. Richmond
6. Hampton Court Palace

CAMDEN TOWN (1)

 Camden Town

Northeast of Regent's Park, along the canal, is Camden Town, notable for the markets attracting tourists and locals alike. It retains elements of its former rough days, especially Goth and punk styles. Here and there, elegant houses dot the landscape, and artists, writers, actors, and media people are claiming the area. Now famous, **Camden Market** (*Camden High St., off Chalk Farm Rd., www. camdenlock.net; hours: daily 10AM–6PM*) features artisan boutiques. **Camden Lock Market** is the most interesting, with arts and crafts, antiques, and products of cottage industries. The **Jewish Museum, Camden** (*Raymond Burton House, 129-131 Albert St., 020-7284-7384, www.jewish museum.org.uk; hours: Su–Th 10AM–5PM, F 10AM–2PM*) covers more than six centuries of Jewish life in Britain. The area has a number of good restaurants. For excellent

Cambodian cuisine, try **Lemongrass (£)** *(243 Royal College St., 020-7284-1116, www.cambodianlemongrass.co.uk; hours: M–Sa 5:30PM–11PM)*. **Café Corfu (£-££)** *(7 Pratt St., 020-7424-0203, call for hours)* has wonderful Greek food. **Mango Room (£-££)** *(10-12 Kentish Town Rd., 020-7482-*

5065, www.mangoroom.co.uk; hours: daily 12PM–11PM) is a classy Caribbean restaurant. For nightlife, try **Jazz Café** *(5 Parkway, 020-7688-8899, tickets: 0844-847-2514, www.jazzcafe.co.uk; hours: daily 7PM–2AM)*, showcasing jazz, soul, R&B, Latin, funk, hip-hop, and world music. Local pub **World's End (£-££)** *(174 Camden High St., www.theworldsend.co.uk, 020-7482-1932)* is upstairs from The Underworld, which features new and established bands.

CANARY WHARF (2)

⊖ *Canary Wharf*
Docklands Light Railway: *Canary Wharf, West India Quay*

Modern development of **Canary Wharf** has changed the skyline of the **Docklands** area and brought a new allure to London. Since 1991, when Argentine architect César Pelli built the **Canada Tower** skyscraper on the site of the old West India Dock, offices, banks,

galleries, restaurants, and a major shopping center have sprouted in the area. It is home to the **Hilton London Docklands (£-££)** *(265 Rotherhithe St., 020-7231-1001,* *www.hilton.co.uk/docklands)*, with its own pier and river-taxi; and the luxurious **Four Seasons Canary Wharf (££-££££)** *(46 Westferry Circus, 020-7510-1999, www.fourseasons.com/canarywharf)*, with spectacular river and city views and **Quadrato (££-£££)** *(020-7510-1858)*, a restaurant that specializes in Northern Italian cuisine. Fine dining at **Plateau (££-£££)** *(Canada Pl., 4th floor, Canada Sq., 020-7715-7100, www.plateau-restaurant.co.uk; hours: M–F 12PM–3PM, 6PM–10:30PM, Sa 6PM–10:30PM)* and its less expensive **Bar and Grill (£-££)** *(M–Sa 12PM–11PM)* is modern European. **The Gun (££-££££)** *(27 Coldharbour, 020-7515-5222, www.thegundocklands.com; hours: M–Sa 11AM–12AM, Su 11AM–11PM)*, is an early 18th-century pub frequented by Lord Nelson, now an upscale gastropub with great views from the terrace. **Browns (£-££)** *(Hertsmere Rd., West India Quay, 020-7987-9777, www.browns-restaurants.co.uk; hours: M–Th 10AM–11PM, F–Sa 10AM–12AM, Su 10AM–10:30PM)*, a British bistro chain, serves reliable food.

WIMBLEDON (3)

⊖ *Southfields, Wimbledon Park, Wimbledon*

Wimbledon, a quiet, wealthy suburb, is best known for the **Wimbledon Championships**, the annual international tennis tournament at the **All England Lawn Tennis Club** *(Church Rd., 020-8944-1066, tickets: 020-8971-2473, www.wimbledon.com; ticket office: M–F 9AM–5PM)*. The **Wimbledon Lawn Tennis Museum** *(All England Lawn Tennis Club, Church*

Rd., 020-8946-6131, www.wimbledon.com/museum; hours: daily 10AM–5PM) is an amusing museum dedicated to the history of tennis; it includes tapes of historic matches. One of London's best children's theaters is the **Polka Theatre** *(240 The Broadway, 020-8543-4888, www.polkatheatre.com; call for showtimes).*

KEW GARDENS (4)

⊖ *Kew Gardens*

The lush 300-acre **Royal Botanic Gardens at Kew** *(020-8332-5655, www.kew.org; hours: Apr–Aug M–F 9:30AM–6:30PM, Sa–Su 9:30AM–7:30PM, Sep–Oct daily 9:30AM–6PM, Nov–Jan daily 9:30AM–4:15PM, Feb–Mar daily 9:30AM–5:30PM)*, a World Heritage Site, is the ultimate in English gardening. With 40,000 different kinds of plants displayed, **Kew Gardens** is not only an exquisite horticultural marvel but also an extraordinary and important scholarly research center. Buildings of note include: **Temperate House**, displaying sensitive woody plants; **Evolution House**, presenting a history of botanic life; **Palm House**, Decimus Burton's 19th-century greenhouse for exotic plants; the **Princess of Wales Conservatory**, a greenhouse with ten climate zones; **Kew Palace**, a 17th-century terracotta brick royal country house; **Minka House**, an early 20th-century traditional Japanese house; and

Queen Charlotte's Cottage (*www.hrp.org.uk; hours: Apr–Sep Sa–Su 11AM–4PM, Oct–1st wkend of Nov Sa–Su 11AM–3PM*), a thatched house with delightful seasonal gardens. **The Orangery (£)** (*020-8332-5686, www.kew.org; daily 10AM–1 hour before gardens close*) restaurant and tearooms throughout the gardens offer meals and snacks.

RICHMOND (5)

 Richmond

Near Kew Gardens, along the Thames, is **Richmond**, a wealthy suburb with a picturesque village center dating from the 14th century. Narrow stone streets meander past charming shops and pubs, while the view of the river from atop the hill is a scene many artists have painted. The **Museum of Richmond** (*Old Town Hall, Whittaker Ave., 020-8332-1141, www.museumofrichmond.com; hours: Tu–Sa 11AM–5PM*) recounts the town's history and often has numerous children's activities available. Richmond Park is the largest royal park in London. The lush wildlife provides a wonderful setting for exploration. And when you're ready for a rest, settle into one of the many pubs along the lovely Thames boardwalk.

By train: *from Waterloo Station (every 35 min.)*
By boat: *from Westminster or Richmond piers
(020-7930-2062, www.wpsa.co.uk; Apr–Oct, 3-1/2
hours, time varies depending on the tide)*

The palace at **Hampton Court** *(East
Molesey, Surrey, 24-hour info: 0844-
482-7777, www.hrp.org.uk; hours:
daily Apr–Oct 10AM–6PM, Nov–Mar
10AM–4:30PM)* on the Thames, one
of England's most spectacular, is associated with
Henry VIII, who loved it so much he virtually confiscated it from his lord chancellor, Cardinal Wolsey, Archbishop of York, in 1528. The Tudor parts of the castle, with its turrets, date from that period, while the more Classical royal suites were built by Christopher Wren for William and Mary in the 1690s. Excellent guided tours offer the best of the palace and its 1800-acre estate. **King Henry VIII's State Apartments** feature a wonderful hammerbeam roof, fabulous stained-glass windows, and exquisite tapestries in the Great Hall. The **Tudor Kitchens**, with their enormous cauldrons and blood-spattered walls, are fun—as is the **Haunted Gallery** where the ghost of Henry's fifth wife, Catherine Howard, executed for adultery, is said to roam. Sir Christopher Wren built the sumptuous **Queen's State Apartments**, **Queen's Gallery**, and **King's Apartments**. Beautiful tapestries, paintings, and other artistic ornamental and ceremonial objects through-

out the palace are noteworthy. The palace gardens and grounds are among England's most romantic. Wren's splendid **East Front**, with its **Broad Walk**, **Fountain Garden**, and **Long Water** (an artificial lake), is elegantly dignified. To the south are the impressive **Great Vine** and the **Pond Garden**. One of the garden's highlights is the world-famous **Maze**.

chapter 10

EXCURSIONS OUTSIDE LONDON

EXCURSIONS OUTSIDE LONDON

Places to See:
1. Oxford
2. Stratford-upon-Avon
3. Windsor Castle
4. Canterbury

Transportation

London Train & Coach Stations

Paddington: Praed Street, ⊖ *Paddington*

Victoria Station: Terminus Place, ⊖ *Victoria*

Victoria Coach Station: 164 Buckingham Palace Road,
0843-222-1234, tfl.gov.uk/vcs, ⊖ *Victoria*

Virgin Trains *(info on train timetables and fares)*:
0871-977-4222, www.virgintrains.co.uk

Online ticket purchases: www.thetrainline.com

OXFORD (1)

By train: *from Paddington Station (1 hour)*
By coach: *(1 hour and 40 min.):* **National Express**
*(0871-781-8178, www.nationalexpress.com; departs from
Victoria Coach Station);* **Stagecoach/Oxford Tube**
*(01865-772-250, www.oxfordtube.com, departs from
Shepherd's Bush, Notting Hill Gate, Marble Arch,
Victoria, and Hillingdon);*
Oxford Bus Company *(01865-785-400,
www.oxfordbus.co.uk, departs from Victoria Coach Station)*
Oxford Tourist Info Centre: 15-16 Broad Street,
01865-252-200, www.visitoxford.org

Oxford, an elegant, vibrant town, has been home to world-famous **Oxford University** since the 12th century. Beside the many colleges that make up the university, there are a great number of historical sites and museums, including the **Ashmolean** (Beaumont St., 01865-278-002, www.ashmolean. org; hours: Tu–Su 10AM–6PM), the oldest museum in the U.K., and **Modern Art Oxford** (30 Pembroke St., 01865-722-733, www.modernartoxford.org.uk; hours: Tu–W 10AM–5PM, Th–Sa 10AM–7PM, Su 12PM–5PM), which exhibits contemporary art.

STRATFORD-UPON-AVON (2)

By train: *from Paddington Station (about 2 hours)*
By coach: **National Express** *(0871-781-8178,
www.nationalexpress.com, about 2-3/4 hours,
departs from various stations)*
Stratford Tourist Info Centre: Bridgefoot, 0870-160-7930,
0871-978-0800, www.shakespeare-country.co.uk;
call for hours.

Stratford-upon-Avon, Shakespeare's birthplace, is an enchanting, historic town. It is home to the **Royal Shakespeare Company** (*Waterside, www.rsc.org.uk; Royal Shakespeare Theatre, tickets: 0844-800-1110; The Courtyard Theatre, Southern Lane, box office: 0844-800-1110*). Other sights include: **Shakespeare's Birthplace** (*Henley St., 01789-204-016, www.shakespeare.org.uk; hours: daily Apr–Jun, Sep–Oct 9AM–5PM, daily Jul–Aug 9AM–6PM, Nov–Mar 10AM–4PM*); **Harvard House** (*High St., 01789-204-507, www.stratford-upon-avon.co.uk/soaharv.htm; hours: Tu–Sa 10AM–4PM, Su 10:30AM–4:30PM*), home of Katharine Rogers, mother of the founder of Harvard University, John Harvard; and **Anne Hathaway's Cottage** (*Cottage Ln., Shottery, 1 mile from town by footpath, 01789-297-240, www.shakespeare.org.uk; hours: daily Apr–Oct 9AM–5PM, Nov–Mar 10AM–4PM*), the premarital home of Shakespeare's wife.

WINDSOR CASTLE (3)

By train: *from Paddington Station, change at Slough (about 30 min.)*
By coach: ***Green Line*** *(0844-801-7261, www.greenline.co.uk, bus 701 & 702 from Victoria Coach Station)*

Royal Windsor Info Centre: Old Booking Hall, Windsor Royal Shopping, Thames St., 01753-743-900, www.windsor.gov.uk; Jun–Oct M–F 9:30AM–5:30PM, Sa 9:30AM–5PM, Su 10AM–4PM; Nov–Mar Sa 10AM–5PM, Su–F 10AM–4PM; Apr–May M–Sa 10AM–5PM, Su 10AM–4PM.

Weekend residence of the royals, **Windsor Castle** *(020-7766-7304, www.windsor.gov.uk; hours: daily Mar–Oct 9:45AM–5:15PM, Nov–Feb 9:45AM–4:15PM)* is a stunning medieval castle over 900 years old. George V, Henry VIII, and other royalty are entombed in **St. George's Chapel.** Other nearby sights: **Windsor Racecourse** *(Maidenhead Rd., Windsor, 01753-498-400, www.windsor-racecourse.co.uk)* and **Legoland Windsor** theme park *(Winkfield Rd., Windsor, 0871-222-2001, www.legoland.co.uk; view opening times on Web site).*

CANTERBURY (4)

By train: *from Victoria Station (1-1/4 hours)*
Tourist Info Centre: 18 High Street, in Beaney Art Museum, 01227-378-100, www.canterbury.co.uk; hours: daily M–Sa 9:30AM–5PM, Su 9:30AM–4:30PM

Canterbury is a romantic medieval town, a seemingly fairy-tale village. Traffic is not allowed during the daytime in the city center, so visitors can easily stroll around its charming streets. The town has been the seat of the Church of England since 597, when St. Augustine established his base there. Its centerpiece is **Canterbury Cathedral** *(01227-762-862, www.canterbury-cathedral.org; hours: Summer M–Sa 9AM–5:30PM, Su 12:30PM–2:30PM, Winter M–Sa 9AM–5PM, Su 12:30PM–2:30PM; The Crypt: M–Sa 10AM–5:30PM, Su 12:30PM–2:30PM),* one of England's greatest sights. The exhibition **Canterbury Tales** *(St. Margaret's St., 01227-479-227, www.canterburytales.org.uk; hours: daily Jan–Feb & Nov–Dec 10AM–4:30PM, Mar–Jun & Sep–Oct 10AM–5PM, Jul–Aug 9:30AM–5PM)* recounts Chaucer's 13th-century stories.

INDEX

NOTES

NOTES

NOTES

NOTES

NOTES

transportation
map